Pray Like Hell

Pray Like Hell

How to Talk with God

Maxine Outlaw

Andrews McMeel Publishing

Kansas City

For information, write Andrews McMeel Publishing, an Andrews McMeel Universal company, 4520 Main Street, Kansas City, Missouri 64111.

www.andrewsmcmeel.com

LIBRARY OF CONGRESS CATALOGING-IN-PUBLICATION DATA
Outlaw, Maxine.
Pray like hell : how to talk with God / Maxine Outlaw.
p. cm.
Includes bibliographical references.
ISBN 0-8362-6772-9 (pbk.)
1. Prayer—Christianity. I. Title.
BV215.098 1998
248.3'2—dc21 98-16740
CIP

Designed by Kathryn Parise

In memory of my mother,

Shirley Crosby

1928–1997

Contents

Introduction

Just When You Think It's Safe . . .

The Neptune Society, a firm that sells cremation services, was located in a 1930s California bungalow painted coral and aqua, much like a Howard Johnson's motel. There was no sign of the ocean. Instead a four-lane boulevard cut through what was once the front yard. My father and I came to arrange for the cremation of my mother's body. As we went across to this modern-day underworld, I was overwhelmed by a sort of cheerfully macabre environment. The impact of the Neptune Society's surreal surroundings was heightened by the shock from my mother's sud-

den death. I wasn't thinking or even feeling very clearly, but somehow I knew I was in for a white trash experience. The question was, could I cope?

Alison, our "grief counselor," greeted my father and me in the living-room-turned-reception-area. She was dressed in a colorful polyester suit and wearing stiletto-heeled shoes. Her bleached hair was well teased and piled high on top of her head. Her eyes were heavily made up, and coral-colored lipstick ringed her mouth. Her acrylic fingernails were an inch and a half long and painted to match her lipstick. She had a nasty scar that cut from the right corner of her mouth through and under her chin.

I was not comforted by Alison's presence. Dad was too grieved to notice. Not that we looked so great ourselves. Dad and I looked like sharecroppers. We were still wearing our old work clothes from cleaning out Mom's things. We were dirty, tired—and numb. In his soft southern accent, my father introduced us. With a top-to-toe glance, Alison sized us up—not a dime to rub between us, her look said. My father had $7,000 in his primary checking account.

Alison led us into a former bedroom that was now a "family counseling" room. Halogen torchères in each corner made me think it might still be someone's bedroom. In the center was a table made of a synthetic blond material; the chairs, upholstered in weak, watery pastels, looked like they actually came from Howard Johnson's. As we took our places at the table, I noticed every inch of the walls was covered in urns. Urns of every conceivable shape, size, and material. There were brass urns, gold urns, cloisonné urns, wooden urns, pewter urns, porcelain urns; there were urns painted with flowers, urns that held photographs of the dearly departed, urns with abstract carving; and plain (cheap), synthetic urns. There were urns to display on the mantel at home and urns to place in a columbarium.

"Mr. Crosby," said Alison, smiling broadly, "I'll need to get some information about your wife to send to the Social Security Administration. What was your wife's maiden name?"

"Shirley Maxine Outlaw," replied my father in an exhausted voice.

Alison laughed out loud. I pulled my eyes from

the urns covering the walls to stare at her. Quickly recovering, Alison continued addressing my father. "What was your wife's father's name?"

Dad looked at me. I looked at Dad.

"I have no idea," I said. "Wait! I think it may have been James."

"Yeah, that might be right." Then to Alison, "Yeah, I think it was James Outlaw."

Alison looked confused by our uncertainty. "And what was your wife's mother's name?" she asked my father somewhat coolly.

Dad looked at me. I looked at Dad.

"I can't even guess her name," I said to my father.

"Me either," he said. "Let's see now, I think her last name may have been Hubbard. Was that it?" he asked, looking at me.

I shook my head. "I don't know."

"I really don't know," Dad said to Alison. Alison pursed her lips in disapproval at our ignorance of the departed mother and wife.

"I'll put down 'unknown,'" she said crisply.

Looking directly at Alison, I said, "My mother's father died when she was fourteen years old; her mother died when she was two. So you see, we never knew her parents, and Mom didn't speak often of them."

Alison's lips relaxed. "Oh, I see," she said out loud.

"Now," she addressed my father. "Where was your wife born?"

Dad didn't even look at me this time. To my horror he replied in a long drawl, "Some *swaaaaamp*." The disapproving look returned to Alison's face. Dad stared at the ceiling and began to recite the names of various swamp-infested North Carolina counties in which my mother might have been born.

"Never mind," Alison interrupted. "I'll put down 'unknown.'"

The interview to arrange for the disposition of my mother's body continued for some time. At the end of it, Alison placed a chubby hand on my father's arm, leaned toward him, and said quietly, "You know, Mr. Crosby, we have an installment plan so you don't have to pay for it all at once."

My father looked at her blankly and replied, "No, I'll write a check for the whole amount. In fact, I'll write a check for my own cremation as well."

Surprised by an unexpected sale, Alison began

the interview process all over again, this time with my father as the subject. And this time my father was much better informed.

When Alison left the room to complete the paperwork on the disposition of my mother's *and* father's bodies, Dad said, "I suppose you've said prayers for your mother."

I had done no such thing. I was too stunned, too hurt to form any prayer. "Of course I have," I lied, hoping to comfort my father a little. All I'd been able to do since I learned of my mother's death was repeat in the dark places of my benumbed mind, "Oh, God! Oh, God!" over and over and over again. But later, much later, when the darkness lifted a little, I realized that this, too, was a prayer for my mother and for all of us. And I realized that God is speaking to us always, no matter how tragic or tawdry the circumstances. Mysteriously, whether God's voice speaks to us in a whisper or even in silence, the message is the same—"I love you. Come home. Let's talk."

Let's Get a Few Things Straight

Real Prayer Is Getting On with Your Life

Good things happen in life. And bad things happen too. Regardless of what's going on in your life right now, it's time to stop whining and start praying. Chances are, if you're reading this you want to learn how to talk with God. In learning to pray, the *desire* to pray counts for a whole lot. Simply *wanting* to pray is a kind of prayer in itself. Because wanting to pray is a way of wanting God. And God, who loves us, speaks to us with our lives.

Learning to pray is not rocket science. Bottom line, there are only four things to remember:

1. God is good, merciful, and loving.

God is good. Period. Full stop. The end. I've had conversations with too many people who don't pray because no one can guarantee that God is good, no matter what the outcome of their prayers. The question If God is good, why do bad things happen to good, innocent people? seems to have no satisfactory answer. And if it does, it sure must be a mystery. I don't deny the importance of trying to answer questions about God's goodness—there is plenty of room in a life of faith for doubt and uncertainty about who God is and what God is up to. But such questions are not reasons not to pray.

To use this book, the first and last thing to remember is that God is good. The goodness of God is more certain than any doubts we may have. The goodness of God is more powerful than any evil that may touch us. How do I know? The Bible tells me so. As well as the lives of countless Christians before me, and the time-smoothed rites and practices of those who worship. All these things declare God's goodness. And because God is good, we know God loves us. And because God loves us, God forgives us over and over again, without end.

2. *Pay attention to your life.*

Paying attention to our lives is the single most important thing we can do in prayer. Living attentively is how we talk with God, and how God speaks to us. Our ordinary, everyday lives are the vocabulary for conversations with God. God is as near as our next breath, and when we pay attention, we can hear God whisper to each of us.

This book will help you begin to pay attention to your life so you can talk with God. Prayer consists of much more than time spent on your knees in church. Prayer is a running conversation with God that happens constantly in your life—in your words, your work and actions, your thoughts, feelings, and dreams, and each of your relationships.

3. *Keep your prayers simple.*

You can't screw up in prayer. You can't fail, flunk, or founder. In prayer, you don't get bonus points for artistic composition and complexity. All you have to do is "keep it simple, stupid." Simplicity is the key. For many years in adulthood the only prayer I prayed was this childhood prayer my grandmother taught me:

Now I lay me down to sleep.
I pray the Lord my soul to keep.

If I should die before I wake,
I pray the Lord my soul to take. Amen.

It's not art, but it was simple, memorable, and comforting—and for a long time it helped me talk with God. I've learned many other prayers since then, but all of them are just as short and simple. This book contains many simple prayers to help get you started in your conversations with God. If you're looking for poetry in prayer, or deathless prose, don't look here. Simply look in your own soul and tell God what's on your heart, even if all you pray is "Oh, God."

4. Pray like hell all the time.

The last thing to remember is to try to keep a part of yourself praying all the time. Prayer isn't special or extraordinary; it is the most ordinary, most human activity in the world. Prayer is like breathing—you don't have to think about it, you just do it. It's like keeping a small window open in your head, or a lit candle in a deep chamber in your heart. It's like keeping a permanently open line to God. You can be praying even when you're not aware of praying. Pray until prayer becomes automatic. Don't give up, no matter what. Keep praying always. And when you forget, or are too tired, or stop for any reason, for any length of time, know that you can always start praying again, because God loves you and wants to talk with you.

There are prayers called chants or mantras and other simple techniques in this book to help you pray all the time. To learn to pray all the time all you have to do is bring your life, a willing heart, and a mind open to God.

What to Do?

Besides reading this book, where does one go to learn to talk with God? Many churches have forgotten that the heart of faith is a life of prayer, a life of constant conversation with God. So going to church may not always be helpful. Then there are worlds outside the church—the social worlds of friends and family, and the world of work. These usually aren't any more enlightened about prayer than many churches. Most of the time it's more socially acceptable to discuss sex at cocktail parties than prayer. Go ahead. Next time you're at a social gathering with a glass of Chardonnay in your hand, ask the people next to you to talk about prayer. I'll lay you odds you'll scare the pants off them and be branded a strange religious fanatic. So where else can you go to learn to pray?

I've found two sources invaluable in instructing me in the art of conversing with God. The first consists of a wonderful string of people who simply pray all the time. The second source is other books, including the Bible, about prayer and the spiritual life.

Pray to God to help you meet people who pray. The best way to learn to pray is to share experiences and talk with someone who actually prays. There is no real substitute for such a relationship. I've had the honor and pleasure of knowing several such people over the years. I've met people who pray inside of churches and outside of churches. Talking about prayer with a co-worker over the past four years has vastly improved the quality and depth of my conversations with God.

But too often finding someone who prays is not

an option. There have been long periods of my life when I've not been in regular contact with someone else who prays all the time. That's where books come in. There are a million books about prayer. A few of the really fine ones are listed in chapter 3. *Pray Like Hell* is such a book. It's written to help get you started in prayer. It is a compendium of things about prayer I've learned and found helpful over the years. Some things may work well for you in your conversations with God; other things may not work at all. Use what you can, forget the rest, and read other books about prayer.

Cards on the Table

It's time to put my own religious cards on the table. I am an adult convert to Christianity. My family is not religious, and I was not raised in a church and never went to Sunday school (for which I'm terribly grateful). In fact, I was in my midtwenties when I attended my first church service. After many serious and heated discussions with an old college friend who was a Christian, I was baptized. Since I had no church or Sunday school experience to guide me in this newfound faith, I attended a seminary and received a master's degree in theology. This both helped and didn't help in my experience of prayer. I had a great time studying and would do it all again, but I also learned that I didn't need to go to seminary to learn to pray.

After twenty-odd years of practice and trial and error, I believe that learning to pray is the simple act of praying all the time. Remember, prayer doesn't just happen when you're down on your knees. All of life is prayer to God, and God is speaking to us in all of life. Every bit of it. Every instant of our lives offers an opportunity to talk with God, which is an immensely satisfying way to live.

Do you have to be a Christian to pray? No, I don't think so. Do you need to attend a church or other religious institution? Absolutely not—but it sure can help. As Thomas Moore writes, "[Religious] traditions offer guidance, so we don't have to be inventing the spiritual wheel again and again. Tradition takes us out of our narcissism and ambition, connecting us to teachers, writers, and practitioners of the past, establishing a vital community across the ages and across cultures."[1] Claiming and practicing a religious tradition can rescue us from a life of spiritual navel gazing by connecting us to others of the faithful throughout time. A religious tradition is especially helpful when you are learning to pray—you really don't have to invent the spiritual wheel over and over to get somewhere.

My religious tradition is a Christian one, shaped by seminary, churches, and other Christians—Christianity is all I know from experience. So Christianity (at least as I understand and experience it) shapes and informs this book. Still, you certainly do not need to be a Christian to read—and I hope enjoy—*Pray Like Hell*.

So What?

I believe that our purpose for being on this planet is to worship and enjoy God forever. Worshiping

1. Thomas Moore in *Gregorian Chant: Songs of the Spirit*, ed. by Huston Smith (San Francisco: KQED Books, 1996), p. 2.

God may or may not include participation in institutional religion. Worshiping God is focusing on and honoring God with our whole lives through prayer. Always remember, God created us to *enjoy* him. This is not always taught in Sunday school. Talking with God may at times be difficult, troubled, or even impossible, but a life dedicated to praying at all times in spite of everything is hugely satisfying and enjoyable. "Pray without ceasing," the Bible says. Pray like hell—earnestly, honestly, and often. And know that even when you give up, you can always pray again, and the God who created you will speak to you with joy.

The Roman Empire during the first three centuries or so of this era was a tough place for Christians to live. Perceived as religious fanatics who were threats to various social and political structures, Christians were regularly rounded up by officials, tortured, and killed. Understandably, this drove them into hiding, and they prayed and practiced their faith shrouded in secrecy. About the third century, the Emperor Constantine got religion—he converted to Christianity, his household converted to Christianity, and, reading the writing on the wall, the rest of the ancient world converted to Christianity too.

Things got a lot better for Christians once Christianity became the law of the land. In fact, things got downright comfortable—Christians now held positions in government and high society, and they didn't have to skulk around after dark in underground churches. Not all Christians, however, thought this turn of events was such a good idea. They pointed out that being a Christian these days was too easy; the new world order definitely took the edge off Christian experience, made it "nice" and socially acceptable. No Christian had to lay his or her life on the line anymore. In fact, no one had to sacrifice much of anything to practice Christianity.

These disgruntled Christians believed that their faith demanded more from them, and so they began to leave the cities and towns and settle in remote, wild places. Many of them went into the desert to concentrate on God without all the distractions of civilization. With this new Christian movement began the rise of monasticism, and the monks streamed into the desert to pray and talk with God without interruptions.

The monks left behind stories about their experiences of God in the desert. Some stories told of miracles, but most were about how to live a life of prayer. Thomas Merton, an American monk of the twentieth century, has recorded the following story from the desert fathers:

> Abbot Lot came to Abbot Joseph and said, "Father, according as I am able, I keep my little rule, and my little fast, my prayer, meditation and contemplative silence. . . . Now what more should I do?" [Abbot Joseph] rose up in reply and stretched his hands out to heaven, and his fingers became like ten lamps of fire. He said, "Why not be totally changed into fire?"[2]

Now to live a life of prayer we don't have to pack up and move to Death Valley. But here, at the begin-

2. *The Wisdom of the Desert,* ed. and trans. by Thomas Merton, (New York: New Directions, 1960), p. 50.

ning of the twenty-first century, we can develop the same kind of passion for talking with God as that of those ancient desert monks. It is a passion fueled by joy, that unutterable sense of being touched and held by God. We don't have to give up everything to follow our bliss, but we might want to give it up.

Obstacles to Prayer

So if prayer is so blissful, how come so many things seem to get in the way? The obstacles to prayer are many and varied. But I think they all boil down to two main obstacles.

"I don't have time."

This is my favorite obstacle to prayer. For me it goes something like this: "Look. I work full-time, write part-time, have a family and shreds of a social life; occasionally I like to read a book. Gimme a break. I don't have time to sit around and talk with God. Now if I could live in a monastery where I could get some peace and quiet and be holy—well, then I could pray all the livelong day without any distractions or interruptions and have a great time with God. But right now, this minute, life gets in the way of praying very much."

Life is prayer. There is no detail that can escape the mercy and love of God. Every aspect of our lives—from the most mundane chore to the most exalted expression of love and sacrifice—can be a prayer to God when we pay attention and offer up our lives as prayer all the time.

I have a quotation from the writer Esther de Waal framed on my study wall: "She has made the mundane the edge of glory." It is a caption to a woodcut of a Celtic woman sweeping her house, an interpretation of the story Jesus told of the woman looking for the lost coin. De Waal writes about how the spirituality of the Celts in Ireland, Wales, and Scotland can help make our lives prayers to God. The Celtic tradition knows no distinction between sacred and secular; every moment of every day, every task, each movement is holy and a prayer to God. When I say, "life is prayer," that is what I mean. There are no such things as distractions or interruptions from the workaday life intruding on prayer time; there is no

time that isn't filled with the sound of the voice of God. Each of us, simply by raising our hands to heaven, can be totally changed into fire.

"What if God doesn't give me what I want?"

I think this is an even more real, rock-hard obstacle to prayer than not having enough time. Too often I lapse into thinking of God as a giant ATM machine; all I have to do is push the right buttons to get what I want. When we pray, we want God to give us what we ask for. If we didn't, we wouldn't be praying like hell in the first place. Trusting God is hard. Sure, we may know God is good. But when the rubber meets the road, can I trust a good, loving God to work for good in *whatever* I may pray for?

In prayer we've got to keep our sticky fingers off the controls. This is the single most difficult thing to do. The purpose of prayer is not to push the right buttons on an almighty ATM, to control God's response to our prayers. The purpose of prayer is to let God have his way with us. We pray passionately and constantly yet hold each prayer lightly before a good

God. To hold each prayer lightly is to be willing to let go of what we ask for into the hands of a loving God. We trust in a God whose love for us is so deep and powerful that we can want what God wants, in whatever outcome God has in mind for us and for our loved ones, even when we don't understand it.

We're so afraid of losing something or someone. We're so afraid that if we really pray for God's will to be done, God will take something or someone away from us. Keeping our sticky fingers off the controls in prayer means letting go of God's answer. Somewhere, somehow we've learned (erroneously) that for our own good God will make us make do with less—less love, less money, less time, less whatever it is that makes life worth living. Sure, losses happen; loss is a part of life. There are no apparent, good explanations for losing a mother or a career or a home. Ask God why? and too often all we get is silence. We get Mystery. We get that feeling we have stepped up to the very edge of a steep cliff and all we are left with are the rocks below and a shaky faith that God is somehow good nonetheless. Welcome to the life of prayer.

To Whom Do We Pray?

The short answer to the question To whom do we pray? is God. A longer answer is Allah, the Beginning and the End, Yahweh, the Goddess, Supreme Being, the Eternal, Master of the Universe, the Ultimate Good, Creator, Father, Mother, Lord and Savior. Whatever name you choose, there is a God. Trust me. God may be as intimate as your next thought or as removed as the center of the universe, but God is at work in time and the world and in our very lives. And the work of God is goodness, mercy, and love without end.

It's perfectly okay to have doubts about God. In fact, it's great. God loves a challenge. And I find that thinking about and trying to understand who God might be is endlessly fascinating. So doubt away; question authority; rag on stultifying religious institutions; give God your best shot. You may have your doubts about God, but God has no doubts about you.

Prayer Is Not Magic

Magic seeks to control a natural or supernatural force to effect a certain predetermined outcome in the world. Prayer, however, puts us and our loved ones at the mercy of a good, loving, and forgiving God. *Prayer is not magic.* Magic always seeks to control results. Prayer lets go of results. Speaking as an experienced control freak, I think people like me are magical people; we almost superstitiously believe we can be in total control of our own lives and the lives of others if only we keep working at it.

I remember my first experience with magic. When I was about twelve years old, I honestly believed that if I moved one hand up and the other hand down at the same time *and they crossed,* bad things would happen. I had proof. If I wasn't vigilant and my hands crossed, I'd flunk a test at school. If Mom yelled at me, it was because my hands crossed when I wasn't paying attention. When I kept my hand movements under strict control, life would be heaven, but when my hands disobeyed, I would cower in fear wondering when and where disaster would strike. This magical thinking accompanied me into adulthood: If I do good work and obey all the rules, I'll never lose my job. If I keep the house clean enough and cook great meals, my spouse will never leave me. If I am the perfect mother, my children won't grow into juvenile delinquents.

Slowly I've learned that magical people are not prayerful people. Prayerful people seek the kingdom of God, that place where God alone is in control, without any help from us. The act of prayer lets an uncontrollable God loose in our lives and in the lives of those we love. The act of prayer lets go and lets God. And what will happen if I let God have his way with me and those I love? Just exactly this—forgiveness, mercy, and grace. Always. Always.

Does Prayer Really Work?

Prayer isn't magic, but it definitely has an effect on the world. Prayer works. Sometimes too well. A couple of years ago I was unemployed during one of the worst recessions ever to hit California. After six months of job seeking, I interviewed with a firm that seemed perfect for me. I prayed like hell to get that job. Waking or sleeping, all I could pray about was to get that job. I got the job. It was the worst job I've ever had. The entire senior management team had the morals of sewer rats, and the junior staff were alienated and appalled. I left after a year.

But at least I learned something: Be careful what you pray for—you may get it. Prayer is powerful. God is powerful. Now when I pray for something very specific, I try to uncover what it *really* is I'm praying for. Before praying for something, I try to peel off the layers of the request like an onion to see what's underneath, to find out what I desire most. For example, had I peeled off the layers of my prayer for that job, I would have found that my real desire was for security. As it turned out, the job offered very little security at all. Perhaps my prayer should have been to ask that God provide for me whether I'm employed or not. In other words, I should have prayed for what I really wanted all along—that God and God alone be my security. Live and learn.

Time to Get On with It

Now that we've got a few things straight, it's time to move on. Remember, God is good; pay attention; keep it simple; and pray like hell all the time.

1

A Matter of Time

One of my fondest memories of my mother is when she and Dad returned my Barbie to me. Mom had called earlier in the day to say that Dad had been climbing around in the attic and found my Barbie doll—thirty-five years after I put her away for the last time. "Do you want me to give her to Goodwill?" Mom asked. "No!" I screamed. "I want to keep her!"

That afternoon my parents reunited me with Barbie—and five large cardboard boxes full of her clothes that Mom had made when I was a kid. I sat on the floor of my living room opening boxes, extracting one elaborate outfit after another. Mom

was an incredibly skilled seamstress. Each outfit I removed from a box was a tiny example of the glamorous fashion from the early 1960s. Jackie Kennedy was queen of our hearts back then, and all Barbie's clothes reflected the elegance and shimmer of Camelot.

There were evening gowns lined in silk, coats trimmed in real fur, mohair suits, ball gowns made of tulle and taffeta, and a wedding gown of white silk brocade. Each dress or ensemble was incredibly detailed, with tiny buttons, zippers, flowers, embroidery, and even feathers; linings were made of exotic fabrics, hemmed by hand in the smallest stitches. Mom knit several skirt and sweater ensembles on slender knitting needles. The craftsmanship was extraordinary, something I was never able to appreciate as a child.

As I lifted each little dress or suit out of its box, Mom would exclaim, "Oh, I remember when I made that! It was when your dad was in the navy overseas." Or, "I remember that one! We were living in San Diego." Dad kept rolling his eyes and muttering, "I can't believe I'm watching my forty-five-year-old daughter play Barbie." Still, Mom and I let Barbie and her clothes take us back in time. I looked at my mother and saw her as a young woman, Mom who made wonderful clothes for my favorite doll. And I believe that Mom saw me as a little girl again, opening Christmas presents and birthday presents, oohing and ahhing over her exquisite creations. For a little while, thirty-five years slipped away, and mother and daughter were reunited to each other in love. And that was the best gift of all.

Time isn't always the powerful force it's cracked up to be. Any genuine reunion teaches us that. To be reunited and reconnected to someone deeply loved takes us out of time, or at least confuses the past and the present. And time loses its hold over us for a little while as we wander back through the years lost in love. That's what happens in prayer; we are reunited with God, who's deeply in love with us, and we wander back, back, and further back in time to our true self, the person God made before all the cares of the world broke over us. And who wouldn't give all the time in the world for such a gift?

Prayer Is Playtime

It's important to bring a sense of play to prayer. Be like a little girl playing with her dolls in the backyard. Get lost in the quiet joy of being completely wrapped up in God. I promise you that playing at prayer expands time, makes full, round hours out of each moment.

In the magazine *Architectural Digest,* the writer Annie Dillard wrote about her study—a prefabricated toolshed in her backyard. Of course she had a house in which to make a fine study. But, she wrote, "a toolshed or a tent, like a tree house, lets you fool yourself into thinking you're not working, only playing." In it she placed a desk, bookshelves, and a small bed. For plumbing she had a chamber pot under the bed, a canteen that held water, and a thermos for coffee. Dillard also filled her study with "all sorts of clutter: bird skeletons, whalebones, fishing floats, stones."[1] *Et voilà!* A playhouse.

The secret to any serious work, like writing or

1. Annie Dillard, "Keeping It Simple," *Architectural Digest,* June 1996, pp. 36–40.

prayer, is to fool yourself into thinking you're not working but playing. God is not an old man in the sky, scowling and tapping his foot impatiently, waiting for us to screw up the least little bit so he can jump down our throats. God is far more interested in joy. G. K. Chesterton once said that "joy is the serious business of heaven." Remember, we're on this planet to enjoy God and worship God forever. That's pretty much it. Play with prayer. When we pray we are like children at play; there is no right or wrong way. Like play, some ways to pray are more enjoyable than others, though, and we need to experiment playfully with a lot of kinds of prayer to find out what we enjoy most when talking with God.

Remember that when we play at prayer, time is altered, because in prayer we live for a while under the eye of God. In prayer, time doesn't matter so much; for at least a little while, we glimpse eternity.

When Do We Pray?

Maybe the question with the shorter answer is, When do we stop praying? The answer is never. Remember, every bit of our lives is prayer to God. No matter how humble or ordinary, every moment of every day is a chance to talk with God—to speak to God and to listen to God. Prayer is a running conversation.

There are times, though, when it helps to set aside specific periods to be alone with God or to pray with others. Listen to your heart; God will tell you when it's time to pray. Besides, it's not the quantity of time we spend in prayer that's important; it's the quality of our prayers that matters most. Whether you have a specific time for prayer in the morning or evening doesn't matter. What does matter is that you pray as though your life depends upon it.

Pay Attention

Speed kills. Remember that. Speed kills the spirit. To pray is to pay attention to everything in your life, because everything in your life is a matter for prayer. *Slow down,* or you'll miss something.

These technological days we think it's a huge waste of time to wait three minutes for the computer to download an image off the Internet. I mean, *please;* what else would we do with those three whole minutes? Read a book? Take a bath? I have a computer game that offers two ways of viewing: "zip," which moves me around at the speed of light, or "best," which slows my moves way down so I can see the details. Since to win the game I have to find clues in the details, slow really is best. And so it is with prayer.

God is speaking to you in your life. God is speaking to you *with* your life. Zipping along at warp speed deafens us to God. Slowing down to pay attention lets us hear God's voice. The Bible tells the story of Elijah, a prophet of God who'd been tearing up the pavement predicting drought, raising a widow's son from the dead, trashing the priests of Baal, and generally being a pain in the butt to the wicked Queen Jezebel. When Jezebel threatens Elijah's life, he gets out of town. Not knowing what else to do, he flees to a cave. There Elijah has his famous encounter with God. God tells him to go out of the cave and stand on the mountain as the Lord passes by.

> *Now there was a great wind, so strong that it was splitting mountains and breaking rocks in pieces before the Lord, but the Lord was not in the wind; and after the wind an earthquake, but the Lord was not in the earthquake; and after the earthquake a fire, but the Lord was not in the fire; and after the fire a sound of sheer silence.*[2]

God spoke to Elijah not with the wind, earthquake, or fire but with sheer silence, heard only when Elijah had stopped being a prophet long enough to pay attention.

A way to practice paying attention is to be mindful, to do everything with as much deliberation and intention as possible. Remember, all of life is holy, and to see the holy we have to slow down and pay attention to it.

2. See 1 Kings, chapters 17 through 19, especially 19:1–18.

Walking Exercise

Paying attention takes practice. Try this. Take a slow walk around your neighborhood. Make sure you put on a pair of comfortable walking shoes before you start. As you leave home, ask God to walk with you and help you pay attention.

Pay attention to each step you take. Let each step be deliberate—feel your heel touching the pavement; notice the way your weight shifts from the heel to the ball and toes of each foot.

Breathe slowly—no short, shallow, panting breaths.

Keep your eyes open, and notice the trees, flowers, houses. Pay attention to the birds singing, the breeze blowing. Don't try to think about anything in particular; let thoughts come and go across your mind like fish across a pond.

Walk this way for as long or as short a time as you like. You can do this exercise any time. After practicing paying attention, you can walk slowly, offering up prayers to God for specific parts of your life—

and listening to God too. Hey, the answer's out there.

✧

Small Is Beautiful

Too often we're told, "Don't sweat the small stuff." I say, "Sweat the small stuff"—that's where God is, in the small stuff. Details, details—God *is* in the details. If we're whipping along at warp speed, we'll miss seeing God. Often the deepest of life's pleasures are found in the small things. You know that. Watching the proverbial sunset, your two-year-old's surprise and joy on Christmas morning, stretching out on the couch for a good nap. These things make up our intimate conversations with God. Slow down long enough to focus on your life. Savor each of life's experiences, even—though this seems masochistic—when it hurts. Because God is interested in hearing about our pain too.

The writer Anne Lamott tells of her best friend, Pammy, who died of breast cancer. But before she died Lamott learned a lot from Pammy about living.

She learned that the secret of life is to live each day as if it were her last. She learned to be more like a child, who, mindless of time, lives in "big, round hours," savoring the small, important things in life.[3]

To live each day as though it were our last, to enjoy those big, round hours, is also the secret to prayer. We speak to God with our lives; and God speaks to us with our lives. We pay attention so we can enjoy the conversation.

Part of paying attention is to engage and relish as many of our senses as we can. Sight, hearing, smell, touch, and taste are the vocabulary of prayer. These senses are gifts from God to be enjoyed. Through them and with them we speak to God, listen to God. When conversing with us, God does not rely just on words. God speaks with us through all five senses. And with our senses we give God thanks and praise. But we've got to pay attention to pray sensuously.

3. Anne Lamott, *Bird by Bird: Some Instructions on Writing and Life* (New York: Pantheon Books, 1994), p. 179.

Object Exercise

This simple exercise can help you pay attention to the small stuff around you. You can do it at work or at home, anytime you want to.

When you can, take a small break from whatever you're doing. Look around your desk or kitchen counter or coffee table, and pick up a small object. It can be anything at all—a pencil, a spoon, a paperweight, a magazine, a computer mouse.

Hold the object with both hands. Take a couple of minutes to look closely at its shape and colors. Take another couple of minutes to feel the texture of the object—rough or smooth, flat or round. As you do this, try not to think about anything at all, or let your thoughts drift through your mind without trying to stop them. Just pay attention to the object for a little while. Then put it down and go about your business—but this time with a little more mindfulness than before.

The Present Tense

The radio show host Garrison Keillor says, "Cats remind us that not everything in nature has a purpose." Cats, like other animals and small children, live entirely in the present. Grown-up human beings usually prefer to spend the present dreaming about (or rewriting) the past or dreaming about (or dreading) the future. Now the past and the future are important. But so is the present time. There's a lot going on in the present. God is speaking to us now, and we'll miss it if we don't slow down, pay attention, and savor the experience.

I think I must be one of the few people left on the planet weird enough to enjoy housekeeping. I know it's strange, but I find dusting, vacuuming, scrubbing, cleaning, tidying, and washing gives me a break from worrying about the future or uselessly wishing for the past. Housekeeping gives me a task to focus on in the now. When I'm mopping the kitchen floor, there's nothing else in the world for me but the mop, the bucket of soapy water, and a white vinyl floor. It's one of the few times I'm entirely in the present.

And I feel like the woman in the woodcut in my study, looking for God in the ordinary. For me housekeeping is tremendously clarifying, and while doing it I am taken out of myself for a little while to feel closer to God somehow.

Please don't hate me because I'm clean. You may despise housework, and that's okay. There may be any number of other activities that help you find the present a rich and holy place. For some people it's gardening; for others it may be knitting, or playing a musical instrument, or exercising, or carving wood, or having a good conversation, or helping others. I know a lot of people for whom shopping clarifies and enriches the present.

Taking Stock

Pay attention to the present, and look for God in the ordinary, small things in life. Get a pencil and a piece of paper. Look around you right now. Then answer the following questions:

- What do you see immediately around you? List as much as possible.

- Is there anything on the list that's important or meaningful to you now?
- If so, identify it (them).
- Let's say God is speaking to you right now in these ordinary things; what is God saying to you?
- What do you want to say to God?

Listen Up!

It's an ordinary life. Wake up. Go to work. Take care of the kids. Take care of the spouse. Take care of the house, the yard. Make friends. Have some fun. The days, months—years—go by in a blur.

Listening to God is paying attention to the most ordinary, routine details in your life. God speaks to you right there, every day from nine to five and while watching *The Wonderful World of Disney* with the kids and while making love to your spouse and while grieving over the death of your mother. This is the heart of mysticism—pay attention to *everything;* God is speaking. There is no romance here, no glamour. There is no need for incense or crystals or a chapel or a solitary life in a log cabin in the woods.

Most of the time we're in denial about God. "God doesn't talk to me." "God never answers my prayers." But God is speaking to us all the time. In our hearts. In the eyes of others. God's answer to prayer may be staring you in the face. In *Journal of a Solitude,* May Sarton writes, "If one looks long enough at almost anything, looks with absolute attention at a flower, a stone, the bark of a tree, grass, snow, a cloud, something like revelation takes place. Something is 'given.'"[4] Don't deny the gift. Pay attention, and listen hard to your life. God is speaking.

Now Concentrate

To pray like hell is to concentrate. Simone Weil once wrote, "Absolute attention is prayer." Focus.

4. May Sarton, *Journal of a Solitude* (New York: W. W. Norton, 1973), p. 99.

Really pay some hard attention to your heart and the rest of the world. God is speaking to you all the time in the details, in the small stuff. All you have to do is pay attention and listen.

Do the Object Exercise again.

This time, when you put the object in front of you, concentrate on it. Keep all your attention focused on it. Stay with it. Don't take your eyes off it. Look at it with absolute attention until something like revelation takes place.

What did this object give you?

Was it God speaking?

Those ancient monks who struck out for the desert knew the importance of savoring the smallest, most ordinary things in their search for God. Thomas Merton gives us another story from the desert fathers:

> A certain Philosopher asked St. Anthony, "Father, how can you be so happy when you are deprived of the consolation of books?" Anthony replied, "My book, O Philosopher, is the nature of the created things, and any time I want to

read the words of God, the book is before me."[5]

⟡

K.I.S.S.

Simplicity lies at the heart of praying with our lives. I remember once being told to remember the K.I.S.S. principle. "What?" I said, thinking I'd misheard. "You know," my friend replied, "K-I-S-S, keep it simple, stupid." Truly words to live by.

Whatever you do in prayer, keep it simple, stupid. Prayer *is* simple; we pray with our very lives. But prayer is *not* easy. Even simple prayers can be hard work, because we can be such control freaks. "I don't have enough time to pray" is such a great excuse. Staying busy with work and family and friends and housekeeping and trying to get some rest and on and on keeps me from the hard work of prayer. But time really has nothing to do with prayer. If only

5. *The Wisdom of the Desert,* ed. and trans. by Thomas Merton (New York: New Directions, 1960), p. 62.

prayer were as easy as finding enough time! What really makes prayer hard is keeping our sticky fingers off the controls. It is the art of letting our prayers, our relationships, our work, our hearts rest in the hands of God *alone*. The art of prayer is trusting God to answer all our prayers—even if God's answer isn't the one we want.

And speaking of what we want, sometimes the hardest thing to tell God is what we really, deep down inside want—because we don't know ourselves. That's when we need to simplify, to pare down our prayers until we get at the essence of what we want to say to God. When I think I know what I want from God, I try to stop for a moment and peel my prayer like an onion. I try to make my prayer as simple as possible.

There is no one way to pray. There are as many ways to pray as there are prayers. A useful thing to remember, however, is whatever you do, keep it simple. I've found that the more elaborate or complex the prayer ritual, the less likely I am to pray consistently, and after a short time I give up entirely. So regarding how to pray, my cardinal rule is to keep my prayers as simple as possible.

Strip down what you really want to tell God. Simplify. Chip away at what you want until you uncover the desire of your heart. For example, take a frequent prayer of mine—"Please God, I want a bigger house. Please. Please. Please." Underneath my prayer request is the desire for security, a place to feel contained and safe. I stop praying for a bigger house and ask instead that God hold me and defend me from harm.

Sometimes the best way to keep prayer simple is to use prayers written by others for certain times of the day. You might want to experiment with the following prayers during the morning or evening.

Morning Prayers

People pray at all times of the day and night. I feel my prayers are at their best in the morning. Because I am one of those morning people. Each and every morning I'm terminally cheerful—the sun is shining, the birds are singing, God's in his heaven, and all's right with the world. My perky early-morning attitude offends my night-owl friends; they prefer not to deal with me until after lunch. Can I help it? I just love to leap out of bed and get a running jump on the day!

Prayers seem to have more potency for me in the morning, maybe because a new day seems like a clean slate to fill with possibility. Anyway, here are a few of my morning prayers. Try them if you, too, love the morning.

I bind to myself today
the strong name of the Trinity,
Father, Son and Holy Spirit,
Three in One, One in Three.

May no fear trouble me today,
May no harm come near me today,
May no pain touch the ones I love.

I bind to myself today.

Enrich, Lord, heart, hands, mouth in me
With faith, with hope and charity,
That I may run, rise, rest in Thee.

—George Herbert

O God,
Give me a mind to know you,
a heart to love you,
and a soul to rest on your mercy.
For Christ's sake. Amen.

Spirit of God,
Use my hands to do good work this day.
Use my mind to your great glory this day.
Use my heart to love well those you show me this day.
All for the sake of Christ. Amen.

May your mercy be upon me, O God.
May your grace surround me, O Christ.
And may the fire of your Spirit light my way. Amen.

Have mercy on me, O God,
for you are very great
and I am very small.
Defend me from all harm,
and let evil flee my path.
For Christ's sake. Amen

Bless this house, O Lord, and let all who enter here find your peace. In Christ's name. Amen.

O *God,*
you are my last, best hope.
Do not disappoint me,
but bear me up
and let me see you smile again.
For Christ's sake. Amen.

Lord,
I don't need to know everything.
I don't need to be everything.
I don't need to hold everything together.
I do need to touch your love—now.
For Christ's sake. Amen.

Evening Prayers

I am not a night person. I do not like the night. In fact, I'm a little afraid of it. Still, darkness comes as surely as the dawn, especially during the winter. Nighttime is a feature of every day. So I get up before dawn. I can face the darkness when I know that in an hour or two the sky will begin to lighten.

I know it's silly to be afraid of the dark at the end of the twentieth century. After all, darkness is just the absence of light. Sophisticated technologies can keep us in light twenty-four hours a day. Fear of the night is such a primitive thing. But maybe it's not so silly.

I believe our most honest, heartfelt prayers are the ones we pray in the middle of the night. Those prayers may not be very brave or noble or holy, but they come straight from the gut to God's ear. When we're lying in bed with exhausted bodies and anxious minds, our usual, daily social defenses are all that's asleep. We are most open to God our Creator, who knows our inmost thoughts, our secret dreams. In the middle of the night, when we can't get off that treadmill of worry and fear, the words "Please God, help!" form on our lips, take wing, and fly through the darkness.

When it's 2:00 A.M. and the night is beginning to get to you, try saying one of these prayers. The first one is one of my favorite evening prayers from "An

Order for Compline" in the Episcopal Church's *Book of Common Prayer.*

Keep watch, dear Lord, with those who work, or watch, or weep this night, and give your angels charge over those who sleep. Tend the sick, Lord Christ; give rest to the weary, bless the dying, soothe the suffering, pity the afflicted, shield the joyous; and all for your love's sake. Amen.

As darkness falls, O Lord, keep your light burning in this place. Defend all who rest here from harm and evil. And let all of us feel your presence as we sleep. In Christ's name. Amen.

O God, may all who slumber here dream of you and know that you are near. Amen.

Be my light until tomorrow, O Lord.
Cover me with your mercy.
Hold me with your love.
And may your grace see me safely to the morning. Amen.

Why are you silent, O God,
and there are no answers?
Why do you shroud yourself in darkness
and hide your light from me?
Only let my spirit walk gracefully in Christ
tonight and every night
until your Word touches me again. Amen.

The fear of night is upon me, O God.
Drive away
the darkness with your bright grace;
the cold with your warm love;
the nightmares with your peace.
In the name of Christ, I pray. Amen.

Thank you, God, today is over!
Soothe my anxious mind;
heal my exhausted body;
calm my troubled heart;
and let me rest sweetly and deeply in your arms.
Amen.

A Reminder

Whether you pray in the morning or at night, or all day long, remember to play and experiment with prayer. Whatever you do, keep it simple; pay attention to your life. And let the time go by wrapped up in the God who loved you before you were made.

2

The Real World

You'd think a seminary student would know how to pray. But when I was in seminary, prayer seemed to be a separate activity, apart from the rest of life. It was spiritual, otherworldly. Sure, I could see answers to prayer in the real world, but prayer happened in spite of or outside of the physical, everyday world. It wasn't the seminary's fault I had chopped the world in two—the spiritual and the physical. Remember, I never went to Sunday school, so praying at all was a pretty new experience for me.

During my seminary education, I hit a very difficult time. I was struggling with a lot of depression;

the world was a dark and fearful place. Faith offered little comfort. Prayer did no good that I could see. A friend told me about a woman who frequently prayed with seminary students and said that I should go see her.

The day I went to meet Joan, I felt like I was consulting a psychic. I was a little embarrassed that my life had come to such a pass that I needed expert spiritual help. I mean, I was studying theology, for God's sake. I should be able to think my way out of the darkness, I told myself. Besides, this woman might be crazy. I just didn't know what, or whom, to expect.

I parked my car in front of Joan's attractive contemporary town house with its small, well-kept front garden. Joan answered the door with "Hello. Hello. Come in. Come in. I've been expecting you." She was at least seventy-five years old and tall, with a reddish, weathered face. She wore polyester stretch pants and a sweater. For some reason I noticed her ankles, which were very red and swollen. I wondered whether she had heart problems. In spite of that, however, Joan was extremely energetic, moving around her town house with confidence and the air

of one who tolerates no nonsense. She was the least mystical-looking person I'd ever met.

"Sit down," she commanded, "and tell me why you're here." I obeyed instantly, perching myself on her large leather couch, my hands clasped neatly in my lap. I tried to look calm and strong, and somehow holy because, after all, I was in seminary. Then I looked Joan in her steel gray eyes. I dissolved. In a weak, shaky voice, with tears streaming down my face, I told her how dark and fearful my life had become, how I was unable to pray anymore, how I didn't think I could go on with my seminary education.

"So," she said, unmoved by my devastating spiritual and emotional predicament, "more than anything else you're just afraid. You've got a lot to deal with, but what most comes across is fear. We'll pray about that."

She paused, sizing me up. "You know, of course, that God always answers prayer?" Joan wasn't at all sure that I knew.

"Yes, of course," I answered, wondering fearfully what was going to happen next.

"Hmmm. Well, miracles and such are just God

working in the world. Happens every day, all the time. I pray every day for God to keep the California fault lines from making an earthquake. And he does. If I and a lot of other people didn't pray about the fault lines, California would be having big earthquakes all the time." I began to think, Oh no, she's a lunatic. "You have to *expect* God to work in the world," she continued, "and that's faith. You don't have very much of that right now; I can tell by how you're looking at me. That's okay. I'll do your praying for you."

Joan pulled a chair from the dining room into the living room, where we were talking. "Here," she said, "sit in this chair." And I did, wondering why in the world I had come here. "You don't have to do anything, or think anything. Just sit there, and I'll do all the work."

She stood behind me as I sat bolt upright in the dining room chair. Joan placed her hands on my head. "O Lord," she began, "this one's so afraid of the dark, she can't see you working anymore. Be near her always. Keep all harm and evil far away from her, and let your light shine to heal her darkness. For I pray in Jesus' name, knowing, O Lord, it will be so. Amen."

That was it? I thought. "That's it," Joan pronounced. "You'll be fine now. God will take care of you; he's already started to work. Here, I'm going to give you something for the fear until God's healing really takes hold of you. Stand up."

I stood. "Now," she continued, "watch me, then do as I do." Joan made the sign of the cross while praying, "The cross of Christ is over me." She raised her arms and let her hands fall over her head, saying, "The blood of Christ is shed upon me." Then she extended her right arm and began to turn about slowly. "The light of the Lord my God, the shield of the Holy Spirit surrounds me round about, so that no harm, no evil may enter to hurt me. For I pray in Jesus' name, knowing it will be so." She stopped and indicated I should imitate her, which I did.

"Now, remember that," she said. "I want you to pray that, just the way I did, whenever you're afraid. I don't care whether you think it'll do you any good. It will. God will protect you." I mumbled my thanks.

"Good-bye," Joan said. "It was nice to meet you.

You'll be all right." And I was ushered out her front door before I knew it.

I prayed the prayer Joan gave me, not just once but every day for the next twenty years. Joan wasn't crazy. Far from it. She saw the world as it really is—a place filled with good and terrible forces at work in the most ordinary lives on the most ordinary days. There was no goody-goody, warm and fuzzy Christianity about her faith. Joan's experience of Christianity was a matter of cold, hard fact, as much a part of the real world as you and me, the trees, the sky, and the fault lines that crisscross California.

Position Is Everything

Prayer has a decided impact on the real, physical world. Prayer isn't something that happens away from the rest of life; it *is* life, its subject and object are the real world. That's why the attitude we carry around about prayer is important. Cop an attitude. That means constantly position your life to be open to the love and mercy of God. The attitude we have toward life—our relationships, how we work, how we play, how we cope with good times and bad times—is an attitude for prayer. We can choose to develop an attitude of openness and possibility with our lives—or we can shut down and deny the spiritual reality around us.

In addition to an attitude of mental and spiritual openness, there is a physical attitude to prayer. Our real-world, physical bodies are instruments of prayer. A friend of mine used to say, "Position is everything in life." And so it is with prayer. What we do with our bodies is as much a part of prayer as what we tell God in our hearts. Whether we are walking, kneeling, sitting in the lotus position, knitting, or standing with raised arms, our bodies speak to God in prayer. So we'll start with a few simple physical exercises that can help us talk with God.

Ritual—Where Body and Spirit Meet

Ritual helps to include our bodies in prayer. It helps focus all five senses—sight, hearing, touch, taste, and smell—on God. Prayer isn't just a spiritual act; it's a physical act as well. Just as there are no boundaries between sacred and secular, neither are there boundaries between spiritual and physical. What we do with our bodies is central to prayer (remember the Walking Exercise in chapter 1).

Performing a small, personal ritual can help you focus on God's love and mercy in prayer. It grounds the act of prayer in the real, physical world. You may want to try creating different rituals that include as many of the five senses as possible. It can be something as simple as lighting a candle or a stick of incense. I have a set of Tibetan Buddhist prayer bells, which are two brass cymbals linked by a strip of leather. To ring them, I hold the leather strip in the middle and let the cymbals knock gently together. A lovely, light, and hollow tone sounds. Tibetan Buddhists ring the bells to awaken the gods before prayer. I ring them to awaken me to the presence of God. When setting aside a specific time for prayer, begin and end that time with a simple ritual.

Hunting and Gathering

When you've got a little time, look around your house and garden for simple, everyday objects that can help your body and spirit draw your attention to God in prayer. Here's a sample (and by no means exhaustive) list of things you might find:

- Candles or an oil lamp
- A photo or painting of a landscape
- Special music to play on the stereo
- Incense or aromatic oil
- A floral arrangement
- A leaf; a small, smooth rock; or some other object that represents your garden
- A shallow bowl to fill with water, flowers, or fruit from your garden, or to float candles in, or to fill (or leave empty) with whatever symbolizes the presence of God for you
- A photo of a special loved one (animal or human)
- A houseplant
- A favorite book or devotional guide or the Bible

Once you've assembled a few things, experiment with using them to begin and end a specific time in prayer. Of course, it helps if you can find some privacy to experiment with your ritual; family or friends watching you might think you've gone loopy.

Begin by dedicating (aloud or silently) this specific time of prayer to God. Then touch, fill, light, play, ring, breathe whatever object you've chosen to help you focus on God. Next, pray like hell. Finally, thank God (aloud or silently) for his presence, and blow out the candle, ring a bell, touch the photo, or whatever to signal an end to your prayer time.

Now let me make a pitch for participation in a religious community of some kind. There is no substitute for practicing ritual and praying with others. Prayer spiritually binds us to one another, infuses our physical world with the spiritual. Although these exercises and prayers focus on what you can do on your own in prayer, I strongly encourage you to seek out a religious community that offers corporate prayer and worship of God. Praying with others is a different, powerful experience of God that can save us from using prayer as just another self-help technique.

Your Jaw Drops

Several years ago I learned a simple physical technique to relax and focus my attention on God in prayer—I learned to let my jaw drop. Doing this simple thing deepened my ability to focus on God and enjoy God's presence. Try it.

First, stop clenching your teeth. I guarantee you're clenching your teeth right now, and your jaw is clamped like a steel trap. This is the effect modern life has on us—just grit your teeth and take it like a man/woman ("it" being whatever miserable things life has to dish out). While gritting your teeth may serve you well in getting through some of life's tough scrapes, it's a lousy preparation for prayer. You are about to enter the presence of God, who considers you the very apple of his eye. There is no need to greet God tight-lipped, stuck up, and pinched. So let go of that jaw! Simply slacken your jaw so that your lips touch lightly but your bottom teeth do not touch those on the top.

Now feel the tension in the rest of your face begin to melt. Start with your forehead; feel the muscles in your brow relax down around your eyes. As your eye and temple muscles relax, feel the tension melt down your cheeks toward your chin. Feel your chin gently depending from your lower jaw, your lips lightly touching.

There. Isn't that much better? Now you can breathe freely.

Breathe, for God's Sake

Breathing is good. Especially in prayer. Breathing keeps prayer grounded or rooted in our physical bodies. Throughout the ages, monks, mystics, and all those who pray have recommended breathing deep, round, full breaths as central to the experience of God. In many religious traditions, including the Judeo-Christian tradition, "breath" is "spirit" and "spirit" is "breath." To be inspired, for example, means "to be breathed upon by the gods." By paying attention to how we breathe when we pray, we open ourselves to God's Spirit moving in, through, and around us.

Not breathing is bad. I spend too much time

holding my breath, waiting for the next thing—whatever it may be, good or bad—to happen. Not breathing robs me of the present and suspends me in the "not yet." Tense, shallow breathing steals me away from God.

I remember when my father told me my mother had died. It felt like the breath had been knocked out of me. Grief literally left me breathless. I felt suspended, lifted out of time, waiting for grief's next body blow. I found prayer difficult, even impossible. Because I wasn't breathing deeply, I couldn't get my body to make room for prayer. I wasn't "inspired." I didn't breathe deeply again for weeks.

A relaxed and calm face can help with breathing deep, round, full breaths. Now that your jaw has dropped, you may notice that your abdomen is balled up in knots. It's time to make room in your body to breathe and pray.

Take a Breather

Find a comfortable chair, in which you can sit up straight with both feet flat on the floor. Now let your jaw drop and your facial muscles relax.

Feel any tension in your abdomen. Let the tension go by taking deep, regular breaths. While you're at it, let your shoulders drop—this loosens up the muscles around your chest and lets more air into your lungs. Simply practice breathing deeply and regularly for a few minutes, keeping your jaw slack and your face relaxed.

Still sitting in the chair, with both feet on the floor, put your hands, palms down, on top of your thighs. With your palms down, breathe in. Now breathe out as you turn your palms up in your lap. Repeat this a few times. Breathe in, palms down. Breathe out, palms up.

Now pray. As you breathe in, palms down, receive the presence and love of God. As you breathe out, palms up, let whatever is on your heart or mind at the moment drift out of your nostrils, out of your hands to God. That's all there is to it. Do this for as long as you like.

✧

Prayer Takes a Walk

I'm a firm believer in praying as you walk. Walking focuses our attention on God while giving our bodies something to do. And it helps us breathe deeply and regularly, inspiring us to prayer. The Walking Exercise in chapter 1 is great to practice regularly. Doing this exercise helps tear down walls between the physical and spiritual worlds.

The Power of Chant

One day my friend Stephanie was driving to the grocery store. She never saw the truck run the stop sign. As the truck hit her car broadside, Stephanie began to chant an ancient prayer. She chanted over and over again as her car spun out of control. She continued to chant as she lay trapped in the car waiting for help. Stephanie didn't stop chanting until the rescue workers lifted her out of the car.

Stephanie began to pray through chant because she was afraid of flying but her job required her to fly frequently. To calm her fear and give her mind and heart something other than flying to focus on, Stephanie began to chant, "Lord Jesus Christ, have mercy on me," over and over until the prayer filled her mind and heart. She had chanted the prayer so often over the years that her response to the terror she felt when the truck hit her car was to start chanting automatically. The chant calmed her until help arrived.

Most of the world's religions have a tradition of chanting prayers. Chant is singing or intoning prayer. Chant's power is in its repetitive nature—a tune or words either sung or spoken over and over again. Chanting helps us focus in prayer. Like a mantra, chant focuses our attention on God. The power of chant is not that we wear God down into doing what we want by repetition. The power of chant is that, in chanting, we experience the presence of the living, loving God.

My co-worker Liz was once talking about the power of chant with a friend from India. Her Indian friend said, "That's why we give elephants a stick when they are in the open marketplaces. Without a stick in its trunk, the elephant will continually pick up food and objects from the merchants' tables. Giving an elephant a stick gives its trunk something else to do so it'll leave the things on the tables alone."

Our minds are like the elephant's trunk; we need to give them a stick to help us pay attention to God. Chant works just like the elephant's stick. I've collected a number of chants that help increase my awareness of the presence of God. Chanting works best when you can do it aloud. Saying the chant drowns out the world for a little while, narrowing your attention to God. You can make up a tune to the words, or you can develop a rhythm to repeating the words. When chanting aloud isn't possible, repeat the words rhythmically in your mind.

I find chanting most helpful when I'm frightened. Chanting literally drowns out my fear by focusing my attention on the presence of God. Although you can chant anywhere, I like to chant as I commute in the car; it reminds me that the kingdom of God is much bigger than the world of work. Here are some of the chants I've collected, but you can also make up your own.

Chants

I trust in the Lord, my God, my strength and my salvation.

Lord Jesus Christ, have mercy on me, a sinner.

Jesus is Lord.

Lord, have mercy. Christ, have mercy. Lord, have mercy.

Be pleased, O God, to deliver me.

O Lord, make haste to help me!—PSALM 70

God is love.

God forgive me.

Christ above me. Christ below me. Christ round about me.

In the name of God the Father, God the Son, and God the Holy Spirit.

Peace, O God. Peace, O Christ. Peace, Most Holy Spirit.

Love of God casts out fear.

Seeing Is Believing

Another kind of prayer is praying with the Bible by using the imagination to awaken our senses to the presence of God. In this kind of prayer, we see, hear, taste, smell, and feel our way into the text. Using the five senses through our imaginations helps us to hear God speaking personally to us. The goal of reading the Bible this way is not to get information about the text or to learn it, memorize it, or even understand it. Instead, the goal is to be led by your imagination to pray.

Sunday school was never like this. Because you don't have to learn anything when you read the Bible this way, you can play with the text. Let your imagination rip. There is no right or wrong way to read and pray the Bible with your imagination. There won't be any pop quizzes. Read the Bible with your imagination, play with it, pray with it, and *experience* God speaking to you through the text.

Praying with a Bible Passage

Let's give it a whirl. Select a passage from the Bible. For example, here is Mark 4:35–41.

> *On that day, when evening had come, [Jesus] said to them, "Let us go across to the other side." And leaving the crowd, they took him with them in the boat, just as he was. And a great storm of wind arose, and the waves beat into the boat, so that the boat was already filling. But he was in the stern, asleep on the cushion; and they woke him and said to him,*

"Teacher, do you not care if we perish?" And he awoke and rebuked the wind, and said to the sea, "Peace! Be still!" And the wind ceased, and there was great calm. He said to them, "Why are you afraid? Have you no faith?" And they were filled with awe and said to one another, "Who then is this, that even wind and sea obey him?"

Read the passage you've selected a couple of times, until you feel the text becoming a part of you.

Then close your eyes and imagine yourself in the middle of the scene. Imagine the faces of the people around you. Pay attention to the time of day, the immediate surroundings, how people are dressed, what they're doing or talking about. I like to imagine the text as I write. If you enjoy writing, you may want to write what you imagine in a journal, notebook, or computer. Remember to use your senses. Let your imagination develop a conversation between you and others in the passage. Let's use the passage from Mark as an example:

It's a clear evening. Twilight turns the sky a deep purple over the sea. Hear the creaking of the wooden dock under your feet. Hear the waves lapping against the dock. Smell the slightly acrid scent of fish and the sea. Fishermen are folding their nets after the day's work; some are already heading home.

Jesus is standing on the edge of the pier, hands on his hips, staring out to sea. "Let's go over to the other side," he says. "Now?" I say. "It's been a long day. Can't we just go home?" Jesus looks at me, frowning; he is not amused. "Now," he says gruffly, "everybody in the boat." Peter groans while giving John a hand throwing the line in the boat. James rolls his eyes. We're all pooped.

We set sail. The night deepens, and the stars come out. The wind is brisk and invigorating. Except for the flap of the sail, the creak of the boat, and the lap of the waves, all is very quiet. Jesus is asleep on a cushion in the stern. The wind begins to blow harder. It rapidly turns into a gale. I struggle against the wind to help Peter, John, and James take down the sail. We are drenched as the waves crash over the boat. I am very cold and very afraid. I glance back over my shoulder to see Jesus still asleep. Amazing! Now I'm angry—angry at Jesus for making us sail so late, angry that he's out cold while we're trying to save all our necks, angry that he doesn't seem to give a damn.

Peter slogs against the wind and through the water back to the stern. He grabs Jesus by the collar and yanks him awake. I've never seen Peter so angry. I hear him yelling over the wind, "We're all about to die here! Don't you care?" Jesus stands up, removing Peter's hands from his collar. Looking directly at Peter, Jesus says quietly, "Peace! Be still!" The wind stops blowing; the waves grow quiet. The night is hushed, calm. The only sound is the creaking of the boat as it drifts without its sail.

Jesus slowly turns toward me. His eyes are hard, penetrating; his jaw is set. "Why were you afraid? Have you no faith?" he asks me.

At this point I begin to pray like hell. God and I have a serious heart-to-heart conversation about fear and faith. Had you been imagining this text, your imagination might have led you to pray about

God's power over nature; or God leading you to do something (like get in a boat for a sail at night) that you're just too tired to do; or God's seeming carelessness in the face of death. Don't worry if your imagination leads you to make up events or conversations that aren't in the text; this exercise is to help you talk with God, not pass a test.

You get the idea. Keep imagining and/or writing until you feel God speaking directly to you; or until you feel you need to tell God what's really on your heart and mind.

Praying with Images

I'm a very word-focused person. I love words and make part of my living by wordcraft. But many people are more visually oriented. For them, one picture is worth a thousand words. Praying with images also uses the imagination, but the catalyst isn't a text, it's a painting, photograph, or other piece of art—a visual image of some kind. In this type of prayer, you focus your attention on an image until you feel God speaking to you. Try this.

Just One Look

Select a favorite painting or photograph—the content doesn't necessarily have to be religious, although it can help if it is. Or you may choose an object that speaks to you of God.

For example, I've selected a brass plate a friend brought me from Morocco. The brass is etched in a classic Islamic design. The etching is nonrepresentational; it doesn't look like anything. It's just circles and squares intersecting in complicated and interesting ways.

Once you've made your selection, sit, kneel, or stand comfortably before it. Breathe deeply and gently. Let it draw your attention into it. Look long and hard at the picture or object before you. If you can, enter the picture or object with your imagination. Live in it until you feel God speaking to you.

As I look at my brass plate, I see lines and arcs intersecting in perfect harmony. I imagine myself in the very center of the etching, a perfect circle. As I stand there I feel balanced, at peace. While I'm gazing at the etching, imagining myself in the center of the circle, a thought drifts across my mind: God brings order out of chaos; that's how you know God is at work. I slowly lift my hands and begin to offer up to God the chaotic parts of my life, asking for the blessing of God's order, balance, and harmony to grace me.

✧

Work as Prayer

Here's a fantasy I'll bet we share: I wish I were rich. If I were rich, I wouldn't have to work anymore. Or at least I could work at something I really enjoy doing, like writing or landscaping or investing in equities. What ruins work is that feeling of being trapped in a job, or at least obligated to it in order to make a living. For many people, including me, it's the nine-to-five day job that gets us down. Yet many religious traditions honor work and view it as a form of prayer. The monastic tradition, for example, balances work and prayer by viewing both as expressions of love and worship of God.

But I'm no monk. I'm just an ordinary person living at the end of the twentieth century trying to pay off a mortgage. How can I, or any of us who work for a living, experience work as holy? Here are three suggestions.

Define Work

Work may or may not be your job. I have a job working in a bank, which pays the bills; but my career, my real life's work, is writing, which will never really pay for anything. My writing is prayer, whether I write about prayer, cats, or home improvement. It is an offering to God of my best, most creative self. There are some times—all too rare—when I write, that I feel caught up in God, as if I'm doing what God created me to do. I am a very lucky person.

What is your life's work? You may be even luckier than I am; your job may be your life's work, and you may actually get paid for doing what you want. But if you're like the rest of us poor slobs, who've got to work a job to keep body and soul together, your life's work may lie elsewhere than a factory or an office. It could be that your work is your hobby—like knitting, gardening, woodworking, playing a musical instrument, or acting in community theater. Or your passion may be in community service—working for a homeless shelter or pet shelter, building houses with Habitat for Humanity, working with at-risk youth, or taking calls on a domestic violence hotline. You don't have to be very good at it, much less paid for it. Your real life's work, though, mysteriously brings you closer to God. Whatever it is, the first thing to do is identify your life's work.

And what if you don't have a life's work? Get one. God's gifts to you are too precious to waste. Do something, for God's sake. In prayer we seek to enjoy God; our life's work is the same quest. If you don't have a life's work, you're missing out on one of life's great pleasures.

Experience Work as Prayer

Pay attention to your work. Listen to it:

- What is God saying to you through your work?
- What are you saying to God through your work?

Work with mindfulness—be conscious of God working through your hands, your voice, your legs and arms, your mind and heart:

- What in the world is God doing through your work?
- What is it about your work that is sacred?
- How does your work link your spiritual destiny to others?

Pray Your Work

Consciously dedicate your work to God. Make your work your prayer. Invite God to get involved in your work. Ask that God speak to you through your work. We spend so much time at work, it's a pity not to use it as a time for prayer.

Here are a few prayers to help get you started:

May the work of my hands show the world your glory, O God.

Lord, may all I touch today shine with the glory of your presence.

Bless all those who experience my work today, for Christ's sake.

Stir my imagination, O God, and let it take shape and form in your world.

Bless the tools/instruments you give me to do your work today, that they may bring healing and joy into the world.

As I work today, so work, O God, in me that all may know I am your creation.

May all those I touch today know the power of your love, O God.

Get Real

The real world is home to prayer. What we do with our bodies and our work are prayers to God. Remember Joan, who taught me to pray. Her gift to me was to operate in the world through prayer. There is no such thing as sacred and secular, spiritual and physical. We are in love with a God who is in love with our world.

3

Journals and Books

Keeping a Journal

"Begin here," writes May Sarton in her journal.[1] "I look out on the maple, where a few leaves have turned yellow, and listen to Punch, the parrot, talking to himself and to the rain ticking gently on the windows. . . . Friends, even passionate love, are not my real life unless there is time alone in which to explore and to discover what is happening or has happened."

And that is as good a reason as any to keep a

1. May Sarton, *Journal of a Solitude* (New York: W. W. Norton,1973), p. 1.

journal—to explore what is happening or has happened; what God may be saying to you, what you may be saying to God. Keeping a journal is a way of praying. The act of writing in a journal forces me to stop and pay attention to what is happening in my life. To write for a little while in a journal, I must sit by myself and reflect on what, in God's name, is going on. Often, writing in my journal about a seemingly ordinary day turns into prayer. Or I begin to write about what I see outside my window, and end by seeing God's presence there. Journaling is a way of keeping track of the ordinary in order to hear God's voice in our lives, or to share our lives with God.

When I keep a journal, I buy a new blank book and simply start to write regularly about anything that comes to mind. There's no secret to journaling. Like prayer itself, journal keeping has no rules. You don't have to spell correctly; for that matter, you don't even have to use words (many journal keepers sketch and draw pictures about their lives). Some writers say that you're not really journaling unless you write every day. This, I believe, is hogwash. I write when I need to write. Sometimes I write a paragraph or two every day, but many more times I write a few pages a week for six months and then don't pick up my journal again for a couple of years. To keep a journal, write when you feel you need to for as long as you feel you need to.

I caution you only to keep your journal private. It must be a place where you can write totally honestly about what is happening or has happened. Keep your journal where others won't find it easily. When and if the time is ever right to share your journal with someone, go ahead. But generally it's best to keep it private so your thoughts and prayers can flow freely.

You can keep a general journal that gives you a place to reflect and meditate about what's going on with your life. Or you can keep a journal dedicated to a specific purpose. Here are examples of five kinds.

The Journal as Diary

Keep a diary in which to record daily events. It may not sound very exciting, but after a few weeks of keeping a diary, patterns and rhythms to your life, even themes, begin to emerge. Pay attention to those patterns and rhythms—you may be surprised to read what God is saying to you there.

The Dream Journal

Dreams are the stories our unconscious minds tell about ourselves. Using the language of story, myths, and symbols, dreams often tell us what's really on our hearts and minds. And sometimes God speaks to us through our dreams. But you can't listen to the stories your dreams tell you until you remember them and work with them a bit.

Capturing dreams takes a little practice. Writing down your dreams for a while will increase your ability to remember them and give you practice translating them. I keep a blank journal by my bedside and jot down dreams as soon as I wake up so I won't forget them. Then, when I have time later on, I read the dream I've recorded and translate what it is telling me.

For example, there is a recurring dream I have when I'm stressed out and anxious. I dream I'm trapped in a falling elevator. As it plunges downward, I become weightless, hanging in the middle of the falling elevator, waiting in terror for it to strike the ground. I wake up before the elevator hits bottom. I make a note of the dream, read it later, and write about whatever may be causing the anxiety. Then I pray for God's help and comfort.

The Prayer Journal

I compose prayers in my prayer journal and use it as a devotional book, praying the prayers over and over again. Sometimes I record in my journal prayers that I've read elsewhere or passages from books that inspire me to pray.

A friend of mine who keeps a prayer journal also records in it answers to prayers. He says writing down how God answered prayers helps him to see God at work in his life. He also keeps a list of people he prays for in his prayer journal as a gentle reminder to pray for them regularly.

The Travel Journal

Keeping a travel or vacation journal is fun. It's even more fun to read a few years after you've taken the trip. Taking photographs is great, but they don't record your impressions of people or how you felt during an event. In a travel journal you can record how you reacted to the people and places you visited in the moment. Let me show you what I mean.

Several years ago I went on one of those "singles" vacations at a resort in the Mexican desert. Here is an excerpt from the travel journal I kept.

July 3

Another day.

Many women with bright pink fake fingernails wear bathing suits that show too much cellulite. And many men and women have strange tattoos carved in interesting places.

A waiter came up to me as I was reading and asked whether I'd like something to drink. I said, "No, thank you," and he turned to move on to

> the next patron. Underneath his apron all he was wearing was a dark brown tan. It was a lovely behind, the only truly lovely behind I've seen since I've been here.

My travel journal goes on, but I don't want to bore you with my account of meeting Nazis from Zimbabwe at the bar or getting severe sun rash or encountering people who were neonatal victims of thalidomide poisoning. It was the worst vacation of my life. I wish I could say a profound spiritual experience emerged from my vacation. It didn't. And I still have absolutely no idea what God was saying to me with it.

The Particular Journal

A particular journal is written so you can focus on a specific part of your life, like a relationship with a particular person or your career. In the past I've kept a journal that chronicled the growth of a friendship. When I was unemployed, I kept a journal about that experience, wrote about what I wanted to do with my life, and recorded prayers for

God to care and provide for me. Currently I keep a particular journal in which I record thoughts on writing and book ideas.

You can have several particular journals going at once. You don't have to write in them all the time or even very regularly. Write only when you need help focusing on a particular person, issue, or experience in your life and want to understand what God is saying to you there.

The Garden Journal

Bookstores now carry a variety of garden journals. They are usually illustrated with drawings or photos of gardens while offering blank spaces in which to record observations about your own garden.

I've occasionally kept a garden journal, not only because I love gardening but because I need to be grounded in nature's seasons. Looking back over past garden journals, I see that last year's pansies became this year's daffodils, that the fuchsia I thought dead in August revived to bloom again with the

February rains, that the little jasmine vine I planted quickly grew into a cool arbor.

God speaks to me through my garden. What comes through loud and clear is that nothing lasts forever; there is a season for everything. The bare trees and barren ground of midwinter turn into a riot of color with the spring.

Reading Books

Books of Prayer and Books on Prayer

Books are a great source of help in learning to pray. You may want to experiment with a daily prayer book or devotional guide. The advantage to these is that you don't have to reinvent the wheel; thousands upon thousands of the faithful have used and refined these books over long periods of time. They offer structure and order to your prayers, printed in black and white. Prayer books come with all kinds of theological or denominational bents.

Prayer books or devotional guides are readily available at religious bookstores or sometimes in more enlightened (and well-stocked) general bookstores. If you have trouble finding any of the titles I list, any bookstore (traditional and online) can specially order books for you.

The Prayer Book Office, publication of the Episcopal Church: Seabury Press.

This can be hard to find, but it's worth the search. It is the Episcopal daily prayer book that includes morning and evening prayer, and prayer for noontime. It is incredibly beautiful and contains all you need to pray every day, including Bible readings.

A Guide to Prayer for All God's People, by Reuben P. Job and Norman Shawchuck. Nashville: Upper Room Books.

This is an easy-to-use collection of prayers and Bible readings organized around weekly themes. It also includes "monthly retreat models," twelve guides for prayer retreats you can take throughout the year. You can buy it directly from the publisher at 1908 Grand Ave., P.O. Box 189, Nashville, TN 37202.

Celtic Daily Prayer: A Northumbrian Office, by John Skinner and Andy Raine. San Francisco: Harper San Francisco, Marshall Pickering Books.

This is a wonderful collection of daily prayers, modern

and ancient, from the Celtic tradition. It includes morning prayer, midday prayer, evening prayer, and meditations—even an order for Holy Communion. I am attracted to this prayer book because of the Celtic influence in breaking down the barriers between the secular and sacred.

Books *about* prayer offer in-depth insight on how to pray. They can recommend techniques for prayer as well as give histories and theologies of prayer. Here are four of my favorites:

The Other Side of Silence: A Guide to Christian Meditation, by Morton T. Kelsey. Mahwah, NJ: Paulist Press, 1976.

This is a classic. It explores silence and meditation as prayer. Combining a Jungian perspective with classic Christian forms of prayer and meditation, Kelsey offers practical guidance, especially on journaling and dream work as meditation.

Celebration of Discipline: The Path to Spiritual Growth, by Richard J. Foster. New York: Harper & Row, 1978.

The title of this book is, I think, unfortunate. Ignore it. The great value lies in Foster's setting prayer and meditation in the overall context of Christian spiritual growth. He begins with explorations of prayer and meditation and includes easy-to-understand and practice guidance to topics such as simplicity, solitude, service, worship, fasting, and study.

Prayer and Our Bodies, by Flora Slosson Weullner. Nashville: Upper Room Books, 1987.

This slim book is the bible on experiencing our bodies as instruments of prayer. Using prayer and guided meditation, Weullner teaches how to listen to signals being sent by our bodies, identifying inner stresses and hurts, to offer them up to God. *Prayer and Our Bodies* is for anyone who wants physical, emotional, and spiritual healing in prayer.

The Celtic Way of Prayer: The Recovery of the Religious Imagination, by Esther de Waal. New York: Doubleday, 1997.

This book is a fabulous introduction to the Celtic way of prayer. In addition to discussing the lives and beliefs of the Celts, de Waal offers prayers, invocations, and blessings, some handed down from the time of St. Patrick. *The Celtic Way of Prayer* shows a people and a culture that lived as though every moment, every act was holy.

The Psalms

Long before there were prayer books or books about prayer, there were the Psalms. The Psalms, which constitute a book in the Old Testament, have been prayed, sung, and chanted for thousands of years, but they transcend time and religious persuasion to speak directly to the human heart. The Psalms are still prayed or sung in most church and temple services, and many individuals pray with them every day.

The Psalms are not inspirational self-help meditations. Their power is that they go beyond anyone's individual experience; they are rooted in the experience of all God's people, living and dead. The Psalms frequently hold up the people of God and remind God of his work among their ancestors. They connect us to a spiritual, religious community beyond time.

Praying the Psalms

I've selected portions of five Psalms to help get you started praying the Psalms. These selections, from the New Revised Standard Version of the Bible, are only a small sampling of the emotional and spiritual range of all 150 Psalms. These few can be prayed as blessings, when you feel abandoned by God, for comfort and faith, during anxious times, and in praise for the love of God. After you've practiced on these, explore the others.

Select an excerpt and read it until you feel touched by a verse or a word. Then pray the verse or word, repeating it in your mind and heart. I like to pray the verse or word at odd times throughout the day, letting it sink deep into my spirit. You can also listen to the verse or word from the Psalm as a message from God. Ask yourself, What is God trying to tell me here? and meditate on that during the day.

PSALM 20:1–5

The Lord answer you in the day of trouble!
The name of the God of Jacob protect you!
May he send you help from the sanctuary,
and give you support from Zion.
May he remember all your offerings,
and regard with favor your burnt sacrifices.

May he grant you your heart's desire,
and fulfill all your plans.
May we shout for joy over your victory.

Psalm 22:1–5, 9–11

My God, my God, why have you forsaken me?
Why are you so far from helping me, from the
words of my groaning?
O my God, I cry by day, but you do not answer;
and by night, but find no rest.

Yet you are holy,
enthroned on the praises of Israel.
In you our ancestors trusted;
they trusted, and you delivered them.
To you they cried, and were saved;
in you they trusted, and were not put to
shame. . . .

Yet it was you who took me from the womb;
you kept me safe on my mother's breast.
On you I was cast from my birth,

*and since my mother bore me you have been my
God.
Do not be far from me,
for trouble is near
and there is no one to help.*

Psalm 23

*The Lord is my shepherd, I shall not want.
He makes me lie down in green pastures;
he leads me beside still waters;
he restores my soul.
He leads me in right paths
for his name's sake.*

*Even though I walk through the darkest valley,
I fear no evil;
for you are with me;
your rod and your staff—
they comfort me.*

*You prepare a table before me
in the presence of my enemies;
you anoint my head with oil;*

my cup overflows.
Surely goodness and mercy shall follow me
all the days of my life,
and I shall dwell in the house of the Lord
my whole life long.

PSALM 37:1–4, 39–40

Do not fret because of the wicked;
do not be envious of wrongdoers,
for they will soon fade like the grass,
and wither like the green herb.

Trust in the Lord, and do good;
so you will live in the land, and enjoy security.
Take delight in the Lord,
and he will give you the desires of your heart. . . .

The salvation of the righteous is from the Lord;
he is their refuge in the time of trouble.
The Lord helps them and rescues them;
he rescues them from the wicked, and saves them,
because they take refuge in him.

Psalm 103:1–5, 8–14

Bless the Lord, O my soul,
and all that is within me,
bless his holy name.
Bless the Lord, O my soul,
and do not forget all his benefits—
who forgives all your iniquity,
who heals all your diseases,
who redeems your life from the Pit,
who crowns you with steadfast love and mercy,
who satisfies you with good as long as you live
so that your youth is renewed like the eagle's. . . .

The Lord is merciful and gracious,
slow to anger and abounding in steadfast love.
He will not always accuse,
nor will he keep his anger forever.
He does not deal with us according to our sins,
nor repay us according to our iniquities.
For as the heavens are high above the earth,
so great is his steadfast love toward those who
fear him;
as far as the east is from the west,

so far he removes our transgressions from us.
As a father has compassion for his children,
so the Lord has compassion for those who fear
him.
For he knows how we were made;
he remembers that we are dust.

Lectio Divina

If I'm not careful, I find reading the Bible pretty dull work. That's because usually when I read a book or text, I read for information or entertainment. The Bible, however, is not a science or history book; neither is it fodder for epic Hollywood movies. One of the ways the Bible can be read is *prayerfully.* When I read the Bible as prayer, I enter a whole new world.

There is an ancient Christian practice of reading the Bible prayerfully, sometimes called by its Latin name, *lectio divina.* It means "divine or holy reading." The purpose of holy reading is to read slowly, thoughtfully, and prayerfully until we come to rest in God. The purpose of holy reading is not to gather information about God or God's people (or be en-

tertained by their antics). Holy reading is a way of reading the Bible *with* God. With *lectio divina* we pray that God's Spirit guide us, welcome us, and love us as we read. Holy reading is a simple tool to help us pray and rest in God.

I learned about holy reading from a book by Macrina Wiederkehr, *Tree Full of Angels: Seeing the Holy in the Ordinary.*[2] It is an inspirational (and easy to read) introduction to the practice of holy reading and experiencing God in everyday, ordinary life.

We've already seen that speed kills. We need to slow down and rest in God when we pray. Holy reading can be used to read books in the Bible in small pieces at a time; to read whole stories (for example, the story of Noah's ark or Jesus and the Samaritan woman, or the events of Good Friday); or simply to read one, two, or three verses (this works especially well with much of Leviticus, parts of Numbers and Deuteronomy, the Psalms, Ecclesiastes, and the Epistles).

2. (1987: rept. San Francisco: Harper San Francisco, 1995).

Doing Holy Reading

Reading

The first step in holy reading is to choose which portion of the Bible you'd like to read. To show how lectio divina works, I'll use Luke 12:35–38 (the New Revised Standard Version).

> Be dressed for action and have your lamps lit; be like those who are waiting for their master to return from the wedding banquet, so that they may open the door for him as soon as he comes and knocks. Blessed are those slaves whom the master finds alert when he comes; truly I tell you, he will fasten his belt and have them sit down to eat, and he will come and serve them. If he comes during the middle of the night, or near dawn, and finds them so, blessed are those slaves.

Begin to read your selection very slowly. You are reading with God, and God's in no hurry. Remember, you are not reading to gather information; your reading is being guided by God, who thinks you're swell. God wants to touch your heart through the words, rather than have you accumulate facts. Read your selection over and over, *slowly*, until you feel God touching you with a word, phrase, or story.

Reflection and Prayer

The second step is to reflect on and savor that portion of the text in which God has touched your heart. Let's say you experienced God touching your heart with "open the door for him as soon as he comes and knocks." Take a deep breath, relax as much as you can, and let God speak to you through those words. Close your eyes and repeat the words over and over—"open the door for him as soon as he comes and knocks." Or, if God is using a story to speak to you, imagine the scene, the characters, the action or events. Take your time. Let the Scripture reach deep into your heart. As you reflect on the word, phrase, or story, remain as open as you can to God guiding your thoughts and feelings. Don't be afraid to let God use your imagination to speak to you. With holy reading, imagination is good; rational thought and analysis get in the way.

For example, as I reflect on "open the door for him as soon as he comes and knocks," I begin to wonder what it feels like to open the door to the Master after a long, long wait. Then I imagine waiting for the Master—and how boring it is. I wait a very long time; I grow worried the longer the delay. After a while I begin to doubt whether he is coming. Then I think, I've been stood up! I get angry—after all, the house is clean and polished, tea is laid on the table (which I took a great deal of trouble to prepare). Doesn't he *care*? There's nothing to do but wait.

I give up all hope of the Master's returning, and I get very, very sleepy. I fall asleep on the couch. A long time passes. A violent knock on my front door; it startles me awake. I try to get hold of myself, and I think, he's here! Terrified, I jump up, *run* to the door, and, gathering all my courage, open it.

Jesus is standing there with his hands on his hips, scowling. I can't move. His eyes dissect me. I am way beyond fear now. The Master's examination seems to go on for centuries. Then, slowly, he begins to smile. It's worth it! I think, It's worth waiting and waiting and all the fear and worry and getting mad! As I welcome him in, I get a strange but warm feeling that he is welcoming *me*.

After a while, you may feel God calling you to pray on the basis of your reflection. By all means, pray! Pour out your heart. Tell God whatever he has shown you in your reflection time. It may be that God is moving you to pray the Lord's Prayer or another brief prayer. It may be that God is leading you to simple expressions of praise and love, or to tears, or to singing or dancing, or to writing or painting or gardening in prayer, or to resting in God in silence. After reflecting on "open the door for him as soon as he comes and knocks," I pray, "Please let me feel welcome for a while. Comfort me with it. Please. Please."

Contemplation

Prayer may lead you into contemplation. In holy reading, contemplation is not *thinking* about God, contemplation is *resting* in God. Macrina Wiederkehr describes it this way: "[In contemplation] we let go of our dependency on thoughts, words, and images. . . . We let the angels carry us. Surrender is the only word we know. . . . Nothing is left except being in God. . . . Contemplation is like going to heaven for a while."[3] When I use holy reading, God sometimes leads me into contemplation. In the preceding example, I surrendered my heart and mind, and simply let God make me welcome for a little while.

Sometimes reading the Scriptures leads me into reflection and prayer but not into contemplation—and that's just fine. Also, it's hard to know when prayer leaves off and contemplation begins. The Christian spiritual life is not about identifying stages of spiritual experiences. Remember, living the Christian spiritual life is an art, not a science.

Remain in contemplation for as short or as long a time as you like. Jesus will fasten his belt and have you sit down, and he will come and serve you.

3. Wiederkehr, *Tree Full of Angels,* p. 57.

Pleasure Reading

Not every book I read is devotional or religious. I love to read all kinds of books, especially fiction.[4] I've found that God sometimes speaks to me through novels. Some novels have taught me more about experiencing God and prayer than all the time I spent in seminary. Reading the stories of fictional characters often gives me clues about what God is up to in my own life and the lives of those around me. God can speak to you too through the characters of a novel, even though they have never lived outside the pages of a book.

There are no real "steps" to reading fiction prayerfully. Simply choose a novel and begin to read, paying close attention to any insights God may give you. Here are examples of how I have read different kinds of fiction.

4. This section was adapted from an article I wrote called "Literary Saints and Mystics" in *Weavings: A Journal of the Christian Spiritual Life*, vol. 3, no. 5.

How I Did It

In *Busman's Honeymoon* by Dorothy Sayers, the mystery writer Harriet Vane finally marries the dazzling Lord Peter Wimsey. I eagerly devoured the first six Peter Wimsey mystery novels, as the dashing, witty Lord Peter solved crime after crime. But it was Harriet Vane in the final four books of the series whom I came to love best.

Harriet Vane makes her first appearance in *Strong Poison,* where she is on trial for murder. She is twenty-nine years old, of rather plain appearance, a successful writer, an independent woman who makes her own way in the world. Lord Peter falls in love with Harriet at first sight and vows to prove her innocent of all wrongdoing. The first time he meets her (in prison), Lord Peter asks Harriet to marry him, but she refuses. She even refuses to marry him after Lord Peter proves she is innocent of murder and the court pronounces her not guilty. And she continues to refuse marriage to Lord Peter through three more novels ("Certainly not" is Harriet's refrain).

She refuses to marry him because she is grateful

to Lord Peter for saving her life, and Harriet wants her marriage to be grounded on more than gratitude. As she gets involved in one sensational murder after another, Harriet refuses to use the wealthy Lord Peter's offers of marriage as a way to make life easier for herself. Before she consents to marry him (five years later), Harriet must find her own way through various trials and tribulations and so learn to value herself rather than see her value in the eyes of another human being, no matter how wonderful he is.

I discovered these books at a time in my life when I was seeking a way to escape. I had recently moved to Los Angeles (not an easy city to get used to) and was working at a new and demanding job. It was a time of wrenching transition and dramatic change for me, spiritually as well as professionally. God seemed remote, and friends were few. I wanted God to rescue me from the job I'd gotten myself into; I wanted God to return me to civilization—back home to the San Francisco Bay Area.

Through Harriet Vane, God showed me that though I may have *wanted* to be rescued, that was not what I *needed.* The fictional Harriet had to learn to live through anxious times, refusing a convenient means of escape (represented by Lord Peter's marriage proposals) from trying situations. I learned from Harriet that God doesn't always rescue twenty-something single women from extremely difficult situations; God was simply asking me to have faith in him and the gifts he'd given me.

It has been said that all good fiction is good autobiography. Books written in the first person give the reader an opportunity to know the character (and often the author) in an especially intimate way. Such narratives are "confessional"; the main character speaks directly to us, revealing his or her most deeply held feelings, thoughts, and motivations. As readers we are allowed to see the very soul of another—an opportunity we are rarely permitted in real life. Reading a first-person account allows us to slip into the character's shoes and live her or his life for a while. In doing so, we can gain a whole new perspective on what God may be saying to us.

For instance, through Harper Lee's *To Kill a Mockingbird,* Jean-Louise Finch's reminiscences about one childhood summer in a small town in Alabama, God spoke to me about the heart of Christianity. As the story progresses, the narrator's father, Atticus Finch, comes to embody the essence of justice and mercy. *To Kill a Mockingbird* is the story of three children and their fascination with a quiet, extremely shy man named Boo Radley, who has shut himself up in his house next door. Throughout the summer the children try to entice Boo to come outside so they can see him. It is also the story of Tom Robinson, a black man unjustly accused, tried, and convicted for raping a white woman, Mayella Ewell. Atticus Finch is Tom's lawyer.

On presenting his son, Jem, with his first air rifle, Atticus says, "I know you'll go after birds. Shoot all the bluejays you want, if you can hit 'em, but remember it's a sin to kill a mockingbird." Atticus teaches his children (and us) how to live with the mockingbirds of this world—innocents like Tom Robinson and Boo Radley, who do no harm and whose simple human dignity makes beautiful music like the song of a mockingbird, and even troublemakers like Bob and Mayella Ewell, victims of grinding poverty and unspeakable ignorance. Speaking to Jean-Louise (using her childhood nickname), Atticus says, "First of all, if you can learn a simple trick, Scout, you'll get along a lot better with all kinds of folks. You never really understand a person until you consider things from his point of view . . . until you climb into his skin and walk around in it."

God, according to the Christian Gospels, climbed into our skin and walked around in it. Inside the human skin of Jesus, the justice and mercy of God meet at last. And through the story of Scout's summer, I hear God's call to get out of my own head for a little while and risk walking around in somebody else's skin so that I too may be an instrument of God's justice and mercy.

The story of *Jane Eyre* by Charlotte Brontë tells me about the wild grace of God. *Jane Eyre* is one of the classic love stories of nineteenth-century England. For me, it speaks of the power of forgiveness, which can conquer anything. The title character grew up in an orphanage under appalling physical and emotional conditions. She is offered a way out of misery by becoming governess to the widowed Mr. Rochester's only child. Although he is a dark and moody man, Jane falls in love with him. Her faithfulness and love transform Rochester into an almost gentle man, and he asks Jane to marry him. At the altar, she learns of his secret and leaves him. During her long absence, Rochester is blinded in a fire. Jane ultimately returns to Rochester and forgives him; intense suffering has deepened and intensified their love.

This couple's turbulent relationship reminds me that the grace of God comes to us through the love of a servant—a love that grows and deepens in spite of overwhelming suffering and long absence. It is no accident that the last words Brontë puts in Jane's mouth are "Amen—even so come, Lord Jesus!" It is for love's sake that God will not rest until he takes each of us—broken, a little blind, but deeply loved—to himself.

I read my first science fiction novel, *Rocket to Alpha Centauri,* when I was eleven years old. It was a story about beings who lived in caves in cliffs on a planet in the Alpha Centauri star system. These beings were telepathic, and when they read the mind of a human being, it felt like "soft feathers moving over the surface of the brain." The wonder I experienced as I read that book has remained with me until this day. I went on to read the great masters of science fiction's golden age—Isaac Asimov, Ray Bradbury, and Arthur C. Clarke. Long before I knew anything about Christianity, reading the works of these writers introduced me to the possibility of another reality not accessible through my senses.

Wonder can take us out of ourselves and transport us into the arms of God. A sense of wonder accompanies every great transformation in our lives. Science fiction and fantasy writers know the power of wonder to transform their characters—and their readers. In C. S. Lewis's Space Trilogy, the character Dr. Ransom becomes a very different man, a man who has seen many wonders and been transformed by them. And in J. R. R. Tolkien's magnum opus, The Lord of the Rings, the hobbits return to the Shire transformed by wonders that inspired in them courage and strength. Ray Bradbury's *Martian Chronicles* taught me that, like the Earth colonists on Mars, I could choose to live in old, destructive patterns or I could surrender in wonder to the God whose ways are not my ways.

Reading for Pleasure

If reading fiction doesn't thrill you, nonfiction books can be read in a similar way. Almost any kind of book, even a magazine article, can draw you into a conversation with God. Make a list of questions to help you hear what God may be saying to you through the characters, plot, or themes. For example, try answering questions like these:

- Why is this book important to me?
- Who is my favorite character?
- Why am I attracted to this character, and what might God be saying through him or her to me and my life?
- How am I like or unlike this character?
- What does this character tell me about God?
- Is God asking me to do something through this book? If so, what?

As you read, write answers to these questions in a journal or notebook. Make as many observations as you can about what God might be saying to you.

Read and Write

Reading books and journaling help us pay attention to what God is saying in our lives. When prayer is difficult or won't come at all, pick up a book or your journal. Just begin reading or writing with an open heart, listening for God's whisper. God can often be found between the pages.

4

Praying for Others and Ourselves

Stepping into Louise and Ed Johnson's house is like stepping into a time capsule. Their home is vintage 1952. Not only was the house built in 1952 but the forty-something-year-old couple have carefully restored it to its original condition and decorated the interior with period American furnishings. In their house the 1990s are nowhere in sight.

I'll never forget the first time I met the Johnsons at their home. Louise opened the door wearing a pink angora sweater and an enormous poodle skirt (the poodle wore a collar and leash). On her feet were bobby socks and white oxfords. Her hair was drawn into a high ponytail. Friends had warned me of the couple's eccentric fascination with the fifties,

but I was unprepared for Louise—a tall, slim woman with bright blond hair. Rather than accentuate her eccentricity, the clothes and hairdo seemed perfectly natural.

"My *dear*!" she exclaimed, in a cultured, somewhat theatrical voice that made me think of old movies. "We *finally* meet." From anybody other than Louise, I thought, speaking in italics would seem affected.

Louise pulled her husband alongside her. "And *this* is Ed. Too fabulous!"

"How do you do?" said Ed, extending his hand to shake mine. Ed was the only man with "chiseled features" I'd ever met. His chin was dimpled, with a slight shadow in the cleft; his eyes were deep set behind a pair of horn-rimmed glasses. Ed wore narrow black pants with a white T-shirt; the left sleeve of the T-shirt had a pack of Camel cigarettes rolled up in it. The couple looked as though they were about to enjoy a summer's late-afternoon drink on the verandah.

"Join us for drinks on the verandah?" asked Ed.

"Yes! *Do!*" chorused Louise.

I accepted enthusiastically, somehow confident I

would be served a Coca-Cola instead of the de rigueur glass of Chardonnay. Cokes were duly served. In spite of the absence of alcohol, I had a wonderful time.

I've become great friends with Louise and Ed, especially Louise. Whether I'm at their house for drinks or Louise and I go out on a shopping expedition, I'm always possessed, as E. F. Benson writes, "of that delightful sensation of not knowing what's going to happen next." Louise has created her own world, and Ed happily joins her in it. But as much fun as it is to be a visitor in Louise's universe, there is a small flaw in it that occasionally strains our relationship.

Louise believes she is beautiful. This in itself would be all right, adding to her already charming eccentricity. But Louise is very competitive with other women about looks. Once when I complimented her on how pretty she looked in a brown suit, she exclaimed, clapping her hands, "It's so *good* to have a woman friend with *whom* I don't have to *compete*!"

Over the years Louise has built a sizable collection of gorgeous 1950s clothing. Every now and then, we play dress-up in them. A couple of years ago, Louise and I planned a New Year's Eve party. Guests would come in fifties evening wear. Louise told me I could wear her jet black, sequined satin sheath with the crinoline ruffle at the hem.

When New Year's Eve arrived, I went to Louise and Ed's a little early. Louise greeted me wearing a full-skirted evening gown of green taffeta with little yellow flowers at the neck. She looked tall and graceful. Her eyes were bright, and she was clearly in her element. I went upstairs to get dressed. Putting on that satin gown was like slipping into a cool, clear stream; it flowed and glimmered in the light. I felt great.

After I finished dressing, I went to join Louise and Ed in the living room. As I descended the stairs, the black gown rustling around my feet, Louise said, smiling slyly, "My *dear*! It's a *good* thing I let you wear my black dress. Now I won't steal your thunder." Though I laughed, I was crestfallen. It had never entered my head that this was some sort of beauty competition. I looked great and felt wonderful, but Louise had to make sure that Ed knew she

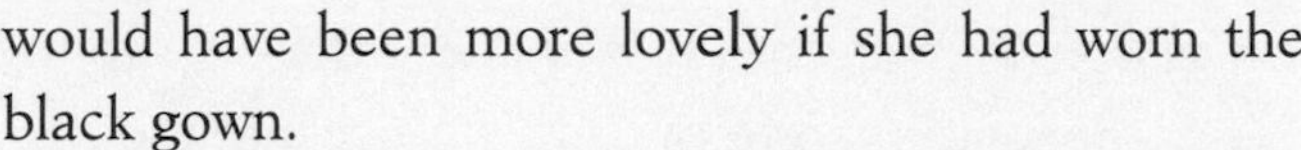

would have been more lovely if she had worn the black gown.

Relationship is prayer. I firmly believe that. We communicate with God and God communicates with us through relationships. That New Year's Eve, as the party went on, I sipped my martini and thought, What is God saying to me in this relationship with Louise? What kind of prayer is this when the friendship hurts? Over the rim of my glass, I watched Louise whirl about the room entertaining guests. And I saw a little girl, maybe eight years old, with blond hair and pale skin. In her pretend world, she wants to be a beautiful princess. She *believes* she is a beautiful princess, walking about in her swirling taffeta dress, looking at me, smiling.

Am I my sister's keeper? For as long as God wants me to be. And I want to put the little girl on my knee and hold her and tell her that thunder isn't something she can steal; it's a wild thing and not for little girls. Besides, I didn't hear any thunder, so there's no need to be afraid.

The older I get the more I believe that being in a relationship and praying for others is the art of hold-

ing people in my heart. It is opening the door to my heart and inviting someone like Louise into the core of me, to linger for a while in the light of Christ. Often no words come with this kind of prayer. It is simply holding a person very still in the presence of Christ, knowing that only goodness will result.

Annie Dillard writes, "I do not write a book as sit up with it, as with a dying friend. During visiting hours, I enter its room. . . . I hold its hand and hope it will get better."[1] When the writing is difficult, she just goes into her study and sits with the book she is writing. That's what this kind of prayer is like—it is sitting up with a friend, holding her hand and praying to God that she gets better.

Praying for Others

I don't pray for everyone. I pray for others only when I feel God is telling me to. There are people with a gift for praying for strangers, world peace,

1. Annie Dillard, *The Writing Life* (New York: Harper & Row, 1989), p. 52.

and protection from natural disasters. I often think that our world is held together by the prayers of those good people, and I sometimes wish I were one of them. But my prayers for others center primarily on those with whom I come into personal contact. I need to know the person I pray for. When I know the one I'm praying for, my prayers seem to have more power.

Praying for another keeps us connected. It's as though we're bringing him or her much closer to us. Prayer is a form of intimate contact in which we are spiritually joined together in God. Maybe it's this spiritual intimacy that lends our prayers for others their special power.

Even when I know God wants me to pray for someone else, sometimes I don't know *what* to pray for. This is especially true when I'm praying for someone in great emotional or physical pain or difficulty. I pray for the pain or difficulty to stop—but sometimes it continues, and I know there's nothing I can do to make it go away. That's when I hold the suffering person in my heart and pay attention to him or her for as much of the day as possible.

The Heart Prayer

Imagine the person you are to pray for inside your physical heart, just to the left of your sternum.

Now imagine your heart's chambers filled with the healing, loving light of God. Hold the person in your heart, in the light. Simply let him or her rest there.

As you go about your business during the day, pay quiet attention to the person you're holding in your heart. Simply attend to the person—let your mind's eye see him or her bathed in light; let your imagination hold him or her lightly toward God. No words are necessary, but if you feel the need to talk with God about the person, do so.

Letting Go of Others

As a natural-born control freak, I'm absolutely convinced that I know what's best for everybody. So

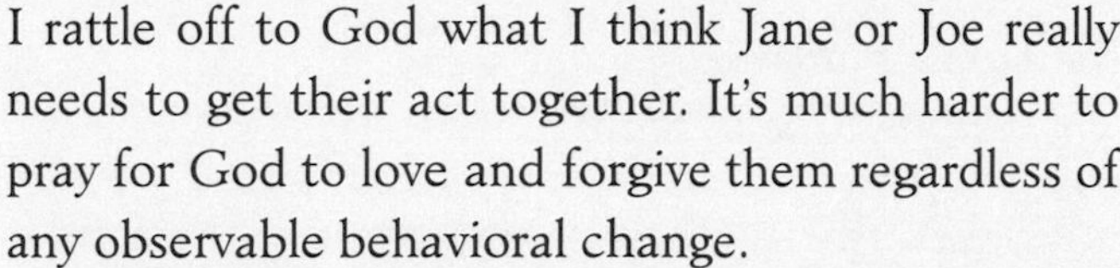

I rattle off to God what I think Jane or Joe really needs to get their act together. It's much harder to pray for God to love and forgive them regardless of any observable behavioral change.

Being able to pray for others without trying to control them through God is a victory in the battle against mental illness. The first and last word God speaks to us is "grace"—the gifts of God's love, forgiveness, and mercy are always there, for absolutely everyone, no matter what the situation. In praying for others, we have to let go of the outcome and let God have God's way. This is harder to do the closer we are to the person we're praying for. But we have to let God take care of the people we love without any help from us.

When tempted to pray as a way of controlling others, I pray prayers written or prayed by someone else. This helps free me from the need to manipulate and enables me to offer up the person I pray for in love.

The Lord's Prayer—
Not a Bad Place to Start

I believe the mother of all prayers is the Lord's Prayer (Matthew 6:9–13, King James Version). You can't pray the Lord's Prayer and hope to get God to control someone for you. I often pray the Lord's Prayer for myself. But when I'm praying for someone else, I pray the Lord's Prayer on behalf of that person. The Lord's Prayer contains all anyone needs in a prayer—honoring our Creator, asking for God's kingdom to be present on earth, asking daily for what sustains us, asking for forgiveness, and asking to be delivered from what would tempt us away from God.

This may be a prayer you learned in Sunday school—and have never visited since. Let's look at it again with fresh eyes.

Our Father, who art in heaven,
hallowed be thy name.

We begin by honoring our God, our Creator. We acknowledge that God is Other, the One who is apart from us and holy, the One who is over us. We acknowledge that God is God, and we are God's children.

Thy kingdom come.
Thy will be done
in earth, as it is in heaven.

We are to pray for God's kingdom, God's will to be made present among us. This prayer is for God's presence in our world. We ask God to make earth like heaven by inviting him to live here with us. And it is a prayer for justice—that the great injustice of darkness and death be destroyed by the light of God's presence, right here, right now.

Give us this day our daily bread.

Hunger is death's companion. God saves us from death whenever there's enough food on the table. We pray daily for God to give us all we need to live, beginning with the most elemental necessity—enough food to sustain life. Asking for our daily bread is asking for God's salvation each and every day.

And forgive us our trespasses [sins],
as we forgive those who trespass [sin] against us.

This part of the Lord's Prayer is where the proverbial rubber meets the road. We link our spiritual destiny to that of others. In other words, we ask mercy from God as we show mercy toward others. This is the part of the Lord's Prayer that saves us from a "me-focused" spirituality. At the end of the day, does grace have legs? Have we walked the talk? Can we say that we forgive others as God forgives us? I can't always answer yes to these questions. But when I can, it's because, deep down, I *feel* the love and mercy God showers on me, and I can hold forgiveness in my hand and offer it to one who has wronged me.

And lead us not into temptation,
but deliver us from evil.

Hey, it's a jungle out there. There really are evil forces that want to seduce us away from the love of God. I don't know what seductions you face, but if

they're anything like mine, you need to pray daily for God to hold on to you for dear life. And I'm not just talking about the easy stuff, like unprotected sex and drugs; I'm talking about *real* temptation, like the temptation to snub a co-worker in a meeting, the temptation to tell your spouse she's stupid, the temptation to flip off the driver who just cut in front of you. Over time these small seductions can destroy our souls. Evil is insidious; unacknowledged, it creeps and corrupts—and we pray daily for God's deliverance.

For thine is the kingdom, and the power,
and the glory, for ever.

The Lord's Prayer ends with an acknowledgment of the power of God. It says that God is the only one who can answer prayer. It says that only God is in control. A friend of mine claims she once got a note from God. It read, "Thanks, but I don't need your help today." The end of the Lord's Prayer lets us control freaks relax in the power and glory of God.

Amen.

The word *amen* adds the final punch to prayer. It means "so be it" or "make it so." It asks that God make the prayer a reality, that the invisible be made visible.

Praying for Ourselves

When praying for yourself, remember two little words—"be honest." Don't try to impress God. Trying to make your prayers sound holy or formal or "right" is often an attempt to hide what you *really* want from God because you're afraid that God doesn't *really* want to give it to you. Besides, trying to impress God doesn't work. Sanitizing your prayers by telling God what you think he wants to hear won't make God love you any more than he does right now. So don't suck up. God hates sycophants. God loves you best when you're being your own, unexpurgated self. Show a little backbone, and tell God honestly what's on your heart and mind.

God is big enough to take it. Tell God what you *really* want out of this life.

Prayers of Gratitude

The best way to pray for yourself is to be grateful at all times. There is almost always something or someone for which to give thanks. When I'm feeling sorry for myself, the best cure in the world is gratitude. I try to find one blessing, one good thing, and thank God for it. Usually thanking God for one good thing leads to another—and another, and another. Pretty soon I begin to see I'm not the hopeless wreck I thought I was. Thanking God throughout the day for the small, good things in life prevents us from taking our lives for granted. Gratitude keeps us in constant contact with God's mercy, love, and providence. In fact, the best way to experience God is through a continual practice of gratitude.

Being grateful is no Pollyanna-like response to tough times. For most of us, the daily practice of gratitude begins at mealtime. For many households this is not necessarily the most serene time of day.

Frazzled from working all day, Mom usually has to come up with a healthy, nutritious meal in less than thirty minutes. Dad isn't in such great shape himself; after the stress of the office, he tries to maintain order among fussy, hungry kids. When everybody finally sits down to supper, Sis is sulky, the baby's bawling, and her brother is trying to tell everybody about his day at school, two decibels above his baby sister. "Let us now be thankful . . ." Right.

But that's where real gratitude begins. Not when life is peaceful and serene, but when everything's falling apart and the resulting stress is enough to drive you right through your eyeballs. For the depressed and stressed out, gratitude to God is a miracle. Being grateful doesn't necessarily rescue us from whatever is making us crazy. Instead gratitude immerses us in the details of everyday life, where God is waiting to meet us.

I once changed careers three times in four years. Each change was preceded by a period of unemployment lasting between five and nine months. As a single person, I didn't have access to another income while I was unemployed. I lived by my wits,

doing some freelance work, supplementing my unemployment benefits to make ends meet. It was at my dining room table that I learned the power of gratitude. There I would sit, my skinny little checkbook in hand, bills spread all around, and decide which Peter needed to be robbed to pay which Paul. Each time I signed a check and sealed it with a bill in an envelope, I prayed a heartfelt prayer of thanks to God for his providence. Gratitude ushered me into the presence of God. Those long, dark, anxiety-filled months of unemployment were lightened by gratitude to God for keeping my head above water. Ever since then, paying my bills has been a time to be grateful instead of a time to complain.

There are lots of ways of practicing gratitude. Here are just a few.

So Noted

Keep a notebook near you at all times. You may want to have two notebooks—one to use at home and one to use at work. As you go through your day, jot down all the good things and people that

occur to you. Jot down your experiences as they happen or memories of good things and people. Briefly thank God for each one as you write it in your notebook. A simple "Thank you, God" is all that's necessary.

These notebooks will become a great resource for those times when you feel down or put out—you can look back over your entries and see all the good things and people God has given to you. I guarantee this simple practice will draw you closer to God than almost anything else.

Say Grace

Develop a habit of saying grace at mealtimes. Giving thanks for our daily bread connects us to God, who takes care of even our most basic need for food. Saying grace encourages in us a constant awareness of God's hand upon our lives. Here are a few prayers to help you get started. (Note: Change "me" to "us" when sharing a meal.)

Thank you, God, for the food before me now. Amen.

For this food I am about to eat, O God, make me truly thankful. Amen.

Bless to me the food before me.
Bless to me the hands that prepared it.
Bless to me a life lived in thanks to you, O God. Amen.

Christ be among us during this meal.
The Spirit be on our lips during this meal.
And may thankfulness to God be in our hearts. Amen.

To you, O God, the Giver of all good gifts, I return thanks. Amen.

I can't tell you how grateful I am, O God, for the food you give me to live this day. Amen.

Accept my thanks, O God, for this food you give me. Amen.

At Day's End

End each day by giving thanks. When you're tucked up in bed and turn off the light, simply say silently or aloud:

God, I thank you today for______. Amen.

⟡

Blessings

The Celts and other ancient people believed that when a blessing was said, the power of God was bestowed. To bless someone or yourself was a powerful thing to do, and to withhold a blessing from someone was a kind of condemnation. In late-twentieth-century America, we've lost the power to bless—except, of course, when someone sneezes or at the end of a church service. Most church services end with a blessing being said over the congregation. But by then, most people's minds are on going home, or the coffee hour, or breakfast, or whatever the next thing is. What a shame. We miss experiencing an intimate connection among ourselves, those we love most, and God.

Bless yourself. Bless those you love. Let loose the power of God's love and mercy on the unsuspecting world. Do it every chance you get. By the way, not only people but animals, plants, and even inanimate objects, like houses, cars, or workplaces, can be blessed. All of creation is ripe for blessing. So spread your blessings around.

Bless You

Generally when a blessing is said, the one doing the blessing raises his or her right hand, sometimes both hands, over the one being blessed. Sometimes a hand is placed on the one being blessed. Then a brief, simple blessing is said in the name of God. However, the one you are blessing does not have to be physically present for the blessing. You can bless those who are far away. Simply close your eyes and imagine the one being blessed, raise your hand, and say the blessing. Here are a few blessings to help get you started in creating and saying your own blessings.

> Lord, bless this child that he/she may feel your love today.
>
> Bless this house, O God, and let all who enter here find your peace.
>
> Bless to me this day the power of God to do good work, the power of Christ to love well, and the power of the Holy Spirit to strengthen me for what lies ahead.
>
> By all that is Holy, bless my partner this day so that all who see him/her will know that God goes with him/her.
>
> In the name of the Father, the Son, and the Holy Spirit, bless to this garden its beauty.
>
> Bless to my cat, O Lord, plenty to eat, plenty of naps, and, at the end of the day, a nice, warm lap.
>
> Bless my friendship with______ so that the power of God, the love of Christ, and the

comfort of the Holy Spirit bind us more closely together.

Bless, O God, all who live in this house, that we may always know your presence.

Lord, bless this computer so that good work comes out of it.

Finally

However you pray for yourself or others, remember always to be grateful and to let go. Being in any kind of relationship is tough; when at prayer, let go of those you love and give them your blessing.

5

The Dark Side of Prayer

One rainy day many years ago, I was working at a church. It was a quiet Monday afternoon, and the rain made everything seem that much quieter. Nobody was around but me and the church secretary. The phone rang as I worked at my desk. I picked up the receiver to hear, "This is Officer James of the Highway Patrol. I have some bad news."

My heart stopped. "Mr. Alfred Thompson has been killed in a freeway accident," the officer continued calmly. "I'm with his widow at her home now. She asked that I call the church to see whether anyone could come over."

"I'll be there in a second," I assured him. As I hung up the phone, I felt my stomach turn over. So,

this is what it's like to be sick with grief, I thought, as I searched for my car keys.

Alfred and his wife, June Thompson, were the proverbial pillars of the church. Both of them sat on the church board and were active in all major church activities. They loved people. They loved me, and I regarded them as my adoptive parents. Now Alfred was dead, and I was heading into dark, uncharted territory as I drove the short distance to June's house. I hadn't known anyone who had died before, certainly not a sudden death like Alfred's. I wondered desperately, What can I do? What can I say?

Officer James answered the front door when I knocked. June pushed him out of the way and fell into my arms sobbing. I held her tight and watched Officer James leave the house. I was alone with the widow. It seemed an eternity, June and I clutching each other, crying. With her head buried in my neck, June mumbled into my ear, "Tell me he's with Jesus. *Please* tell me he's with Jesus." Over and over again she pleaded with me to tell her. "Of course he's with Jesus," I said quietly, tears streaming down my face,

"Of course Alfred's with Jesus." And I prayed to God it was true.

There can be a lot of dark times in life. Anyone who is serious about praying all the time will someday have to pray through a dark, painful time. When we pray through dark times, we don't behave like Rebecca of Sunnybrook Farm and put a shiny gloss on the darkness. In prayer we wrestle with God in the dark, demand an answer, and beg for peace. In prayer we recognize that evil is afoot in the world and ask for God's mercy and protection. In prayer we struggle with our own sin and shame, and long for God's healing forgiveness.

Prayers of Protection

One day my friend Susan was walking home after a particularly rotten day at her job as a social worker. She was frustrated and tired, and felt very fragile. All Susan wanted to do was go home and lock the door against the world. Before she could make it, though, a homeless person who was clearly mentally ill lurched toward her. He was screaming obscenities and weaving wildly across the sidewalk. There was no way to avoid him. Susan just knew that an encounter with the man would trigger a breakdown of some kind in herself. She began to pray, "God, don't let him come near me." At that moment another man walked up to the crazy person, took him gently by the arm, and started to talk softly to him. The homeless man quieted down, and Susan walked by untroubled. To this day she claims that the man who seemed to come from nowhere was an angel sent by God to protect her. She may very well be right.

While I may want to live in harmony with my world, a lot of my world doesn't necessarily want to live in harmony with me. I'm not paranoid—*really*—but I believe the dark side of mother nature (I live in earthquake country) and dark forces operating in a lot of otherwise decent people (like some people at work) are out to get me.

The ancient Celts felt the same kind of benign paranoia. They prayed for God to protect them from harm and evil, whether natural or human. This is a good thing to do on a regular basis, even in contemporary American society. In spite of all the technological marvels we live with, harm and evil can strike us from without and from within. Like Susan, we need to pray for God's protection, regardless of harm's source.

Shame, Sin, and Humility

There is a lot that can harm us from within. Shame has gotten a bad rap in recent years. Many books have been written lately claiming that any feeling of shame is a bad thing and that none of us deserves to experience shame. It's true that the feelings of shame that may result from perpetually thinking, I am worthless pond scum, are self-abuse tinged with narcissism. However, there is a healthy, literally a redeeming, side to shame. Shame—that burning on the cheeks, that sudden, visceral impulse to run and hide—can save us from denial when we hurt ourselves or someone else. Shame makes us pony up to our responsibility for the pain we loose on ourselves and the world. Shame makes us confront our sins.

I was once called on the carpet at work for yelling at someone. Okay, so I used some bad language too. Instinct immediately urged me to justify my action, then deny that I had really done anything wrong. But, luckily, shame kicked in. I was mortified by my behavior. As painful as it was, I listened to what shame had to teach me about the incident. And it had plenty—like shattering the illusion that I'm perfect and in control; like showing me I have this amazing power to hurt others; like exposing the lie that *my* work and *my* time are so important they're worth hurting others. Shame made me confront my well-developed talent for sin—and beg God for forgiveness.

So what does sin have to do with prayer? Confession, I'm afraid, *is* good for the soul. Confession of sin is a cornerstone of prayer. Without it, there is no fresh start, no forward movement on the journey to being human. But taking responsibility for our sins under the eye of God isn't just good self-help—it is liberating. Confessing our sins to God frees us from having to do God's work all the time. Confession lets us be human beings and lets God be God.

The Prayer of Examen

It is because we pray to a good, merciful, forgiving God that we can make a prayer of *examen,* the Latin word for "examine." According to the American Heritage Dictionary, it means to inspect in detail or to observe or analyze carefully. The subject of the prayer of examen is ourselves. We inspect our lives in detail, observe our lives under the eye of a loving, forgiving God. Examen is a taking stock, a reality check in which we offer all of what we find to God.

Our examination will most likely turn up a need to confess our sins before God. But the prayer of examen isn't only a prayer of confession. This prayer can show us all that is good in life and give us reason to be thankful. The prayer of examen helps us pay attention to God at work in our lives.

Take a couple of days to pray the prayer of examen. Inspect every detail of your life—your relationships, your actions, your work, your heart, your desires. And as you do so, offer up to God all the

good, the bad, and the ugly you find, knowing that with God there is healing, forgiveness, and joy.

Begin with the following prayer:

God, let me see my life through your eyes.
Give me courage to claim my sins,
and in humility let me gently lead them to your mercy.
Give me strength to touch any pain I find,
and in faith let me hold up old wounds to your healing light.
Give me wisdom to see all that is good and holy,
and in joy let me give thanks for your gifts.
And may your Spirit keep me company. Amen.

Using a blank book, keep a log for these days. Record in as much detail as you can what you are doing, thinking, and feeling. Write about those people you love and those you don't, and how God fits into your life and relationships. Imagine you are writing under the eye of God. And pray like hell about what you find.

Sometimes the Enemy Is Me

The saying is true: "I have seen the enemy—and they is us." Our worst threat to faith and happiness is ourselves. Sure, there are maniacs out there and plenty of people who excel at doing mean and vicious things. But on a daily, moment-to-moment basis, nobody can beat our own capacity for self-deception and self-destruction.

I try never to underestimate my power to screw things up. And for protection from that innate power, I need God's help. I have found two short prayers throughout the day invaluable in dealing with this self-defeating tendency.

> God, please keep me from doing something stupid.
>
> O God, defend me from myself.

The beauty of these prayers is that they are truthful, simple, and memorable. When I pray them, I find God intervening, touching my mind and heart, helping me to step back for a minute before I commit myself to an action I may regret later. I try to let these prayers live and breathe in a special place in my heart each day. I know it's time to pray them when I am tempted to blame the environment, my upbringing, the devil, or someone else for any difficulties I experience.

Prayers for protection, like charity, begin at home. Besides praying for God to protect you from harm and evil on the outside, ask God's protection from the harm that can come from within.

Angry Prayer

Prayer isn't always nice. Occasionally I get pissed off at God. Big time. This usually consists of long periods in which I give God the cold shoulder. I carry my head high and, through stony silence, withdraw my love in the hope that God will feel how upset I am. I boycott religious services. I'm not sure what God feels when I'm angry with him, but I've learned over the years that God is big and strong enough to take care of himself when faced with my wrath. And I've found God has the annoying, superior ability to love me even when I'm not on speaking terms with him.

Getting angry with God is okay. If you need further permission to let loose at God, read the Book of Job in the Bible. Getting angry is part of being human. We get really angry with those we love—because they're the ones who matter most to us. Expressing anger is part of every important relationship. It's all right to pray out our anger at God, who is full of mercy toward us.

While my M.O. in getting angry with God is to maintain a tense and unhealthy silence, friends have shared with me other, more passionate ways to express anger to God. I pass these along, hoping you might find them helpful ways to pray your anger.

Scream and Yell

Take your car to a drive-through car wash. When the water and brushes start to work, scream your anger at God. Let loose. Give God a piece of your mind. Call God names. No one can hear you—the car wash machinery covers up all yelling. Just get whatever's eating at you off your chest.

Exercise

Exercise hard, preferably alone. I know people who run or walk briskly every day. They pray their anger as they pound along. These people let their feet do the talking. The same thing can be done at a gym, using exercise equipment. Let your routine express the anger you have at God; dedicate your exercise time to it. Pour your anger at God into moving prayer with your body.

Cry

Go into your room, close the door, and have, as a friend of mine puts it, "a complete meltdown." Cry into a pillow. Pound your fists on the bed. Move God with your angry tears. Threaten. Whine. Manipulate. Bargain. Do whatever it takes to make God listen to how angry and hurt you are.

Doubt

Go ahead, doubt the love of God. Question God's intentions and sense of justice. Distrust God's existence. A particularly helpful way to doubt is to write in a journal. Writing is a subversive activity, used by some of the most justifiably angry people I know. Put your doubts on paper. List all the things you no longer believe about God, and let God deal with it.

Wrestling with God

As you can see, the life of prayer is not all sweetness and light. There is a dark side for everyone who prays. While this dark side of prayer may include angry feelings, it is a darkness that is bigger than anger. Everyone who prays all the time eventually stumbles into this dark night—suddenly the thrill is gone. It feels as though God is gone, or at least as though God is playing the devil's advocate. And you are left

in the dark to wrestle alone with God. But this is not a bad thing. It just means that you have reached a point in the life of prayer when you come face-to-face with Mystery, with your God Who Is Unknowable; a place where there are no easy answers, only paradox and strangeness.

One of my favorite Bible stories is the story of Jacob wrestling with—what? a man? an angel? God?—at night. The text is ancient, mysterious, and dark. But the end of the story reveals that the being Jacob wrestled with is somehow God.

> *[At night] Jacob was left alone; and a man wrestled with him until daybreak. When the man saw that he did not prevail against Jacob, he struck him on the hip socket; and Jacob's hip was put out of joint as he wrestled with him. Then he said, "Let me go, for the day is breaking." But Jacob said, "I will not let you go, unless you bless me." So he said to him, "What is your name?" And he said, "Jacob." Then the man said, "You shall no longer be called Jacob, but Israel [which means "the one who has striven with God" or "God*

strives"], for you have striven with God and with humans, and have prevailed." Then Jacob asked him, "Please tell me your name." But he said, "Why is it that you ask my name?" And there he blessed him. So Jacob called the place Penuel, saying, "For I have seen God face to face, and yet my life is preserved." The sun rose upon him as he passed Penuel, limping because of his hip.[1]

Wrestling with God is not a bad thing—you can wrangle a blessing out of the experience. But beware; it will also leave you limping. No one I know who wrestles with God remains untouched. It is a wounding experience that is always, in some mysterious way, also blessing, transforming. When we wrestle with God, something is always taken away, and, if we can hang on for dear life long enough, something is always given too.

You know you've got a hammerlock on God when you've got good reason to doubt:

1. Genesis 32:24–31 (New Revised Standard Version).

God's goodness

God's love

God's mercy

God's presence

God's existence

I said you've got good reason: Maybe you're dealing with the sudden death of a loved one, or you're abandoned in a spiritual wasteland, or you're so lonely you think it'll kill you, or you've lost everything in a fire, or your child has just been diagnosed with stage 3 cancer, or your spouse doesn't love you anymore, or life has lost all meaning for you. You've entered the spiritual Twilight Zone.

Wrestle with God. Don't give up praying somewhere deep inside yourself, even if your prayers are silence. Doubt like crazy. Tell God he's full of it. Pray like hell. Demand a blessing. Hang on. Don't let go until you get some satisfaction. In spite of what happens, good or bad, in spite of even death itself, there will be a blessing waiting for you as mysterious and darkly beautiful as our God. You may not know what it is for a long time, but the blessing will be there—just keep screaming for it.

There is a psalm to pray as you wrestle with God. It is Psalm 88, the only one of the Psalms that offers no hope, comfort, light, or salvation from God. Some editions of the New Revised Standard Version of the Bible entitle Psalm 88 "A Complaint to God." It certainly is a complaint; the psalmist pulls no punches. It is a prayer of the darkness. If you're short on material, use this psalm to wrestle with God.

> *O Lord, God of my salvation,*
> *when, at night, I cry out in your presence,*
> *let my prayer come before you;*
> *incline your ear to my cry.*
>
> *For my soul is full of troubles,*
> *and my life draws near to Sheol.*
> *I am counted among those who go down to the Pit;*
> *I am like those who have no help,*
> *like those forsaken among the dead,*
> *like the slain that lie in the grave,*
> *like those whom you remember no more,*
> *for they are cut off from your hand.*

You have put me in the depths of the Pit,
in the regions dark and deep.
Your wrath lies heavy upon me,
and you overwhelm me with all your waves.

You have caused my companions to shun me;
you have made me a thing of horror to them.
I am shut in so that I cannot escape;
my eye grows dim through sorrow.
Every day I call on you, O Lord;
I spread out my hands to you.
Do you work wonders for the dead?
Do the shades rise up to praise you?
Is your steadfast love declared in the grave,
or your faithfulness in Abaddon?
Are your wonders known in the darkness,
or your saving help in the land of forgetfulness?

But I, O Lord, cry out to you;
in the morning my prayer comes before you.
O Lord, why do you cast me off?
Why do you hide your face from me?
Wretched and close to death from my youth up,
I suffer your terrors; I am desperate.

Your wrath has swept over me;
your dread assaults destroy me.
They surround me like a flood all day long;
from all sides they close in on me.
You have caused friend and neighbor to shun me;
my companions are in darkness.

A final story from the desert fathers demonstrates why wrestling with God is a good thing:

> A monk prayed to God to remove all his passions, which God did. The monk went to one of the elder monks and said, "You see before you a man who is completely at rest and has no more temptations." The elder said, "Go and pray to the Lord to command some struggle to be stirred up in you, for the soul is matured only in battles." And when the temptations started up again he did not pray that the struggle be taken away from him, but only said, "Lord, give me strength to get through the fight."[2]

2. *The Wisdom of the Desert,* ed. and trans. by Thomas Merton (New York: New Directions, 1960), pp. 56–57.

Pay attention to the darkness; live with it; rail against it—there's a lot to learn there about yourself and God. In the midst of battle, you may find a passion for prayer you never thought you had.

Adios

When I began this book, I never intended to leave the reader in the dark. But that is just where I am leaving you. I hope you've got many more questions about living a prayerful life than this book can give answers for. Remember that in dealing with God there are precious few answers; there are only glimmers of Someone and a whispering of your name in the night. But that is enough, and more than enough, to talk with God.